I0592803

THE SKY OVER BRIGADIER
STATION

SARAH WILLIAMS

Serenade Publishing

Copyright © 2018 by Sarah Williams

All rights reserved. No part of this publication may be reproduced, distributed or transmitted in any form or by any means, without prior written permission.

Publisher's Note: This is a work of fiction. Names, characters, places, and incidents are a product of the author's imagination. Locales and public names are sometimes used for atmospheric purposes. Any resemblance to actual people, living or dead, or to businesses, companies, events, institutions, or locales is completely coincidental.

Cover design: Lana Pecherczyk.

The Sky Over Brigadier Station / Sarah Williams. – 2nd ed. AUS English.

Serenade Publishing
www.serenadepublishing.com

ALSO BY SARAH WILLIAMS

Brigadier Station Series:

The Brothers of Brigadier Station

The Sky over Brigadier Station

The Legacies of Brigadier Station

The Outback Governess (A Sweet Outback Novella)

Christmas at Brigadier Station (An Outback Christmas)

Heart of the Hinterland Series:

The Dairy Farmer's Daughter

For more information visit:

www.sarahwilliamsauthor.com

SARAH WILLIAMS

LOVE STORIES THAT WILL ROPE YOU IN

To my husband,
For keeping me grounded and inspired.

CHAPTER 1

"You can't blackmail me into coming back." Noah McGuire ran his hand through his hair in frustration. His mother still had the power to make him feel like a naughty child; he hated her for it, among other things.

"It's been ten years, Noah. He's dead—has been for a long time." Harriet's voice resonated shakily down the phone line. "It's time you came home."

"It's not my home anymore." He had turned his back on Brigadier Station and the whole of Australia many years ago, and had never looked back. There was nothing but bad blood and awful memories left for him there.

"It'll be different now. Lachie's grown up and Darcy's getting married."

Lachie wasn't his favourite brother at the best of times —they'd never been close, not even as children. Lachie was the main reason Noah didn't want to return to the family station. And he suspected his brother wouldn't be too keen on the idea either. Lachie had always been spoilt and had seemed to enjoy bullying his youngest brother.

While Darcy, the middle son, was friendly and caring. He always had Noah's back. Darcy had been his protector against the bullying. Against the pain.

Then both his brothers had gone away to boarding school and Noah had been left to fend for himself. His mother had been in no state to protect him from his father.

"I understand you've made a life for yourself in New Zealand, and I'm so proud of all you have achieved." Harriet's voice turned pleading. "Please, just come for the wedding and look after Darcy's station while they're on their honeymoon. Four weeks. That's all. Then you can have the money." She fell silent as if holding her breath.

Four weeks. It felt like a lifetime—but was staying here really any better? Jade had moved on from him and it was becoming almost unbearable to see her so happy, so in love with Kahu.

After their separation, Noah had so easily been shifted from boyfriend to employee on the farm. After almost a decade of family dinners and summer holidays at the beach with Jade's parents, he was suddenly sleeping in the shearers' quarters and eating cold baked beans at every meal.

He should have seen their break-up coming. Looking back, it had been months or even years since he had made her laugh. Since they had talked about their dreams for the future, rather than just their everyday routines. They weren't teenagers anymore. Jade had wanted more, deserved more than just the hesitant, unambitious man he had become.

Now she had her big, burly Maori warrior. The retired All Black had money and land, and was a genuinely nice bloke. Noah couldn't help but begrudgingly like his replacement. Besides, Kahu made Jade deliriously happy. And after all these years, that was what Noah wanted most for his first love.

It was hard to watch though. Plus, with the farm coming into the quiet wintertime, Noah wasn't essential to the running of the Otago property. Until spring lambing started, he was sitting here twiddling his thumbs and watching his bank account diminish.

The advance of his inheritance his mother was offering would certainly settle the debt on his credit card, and maybe even help him put a deposit on his own place.

"Four weeks?"

"Four weeks. I'll pay for your flights and at the end of the month I'll give you everything you're owed," Harriet said.

"Then that's it? You promise you won't ask anymore of me?"

"I promise." Her voice lifted with the hint of a smile.

"Fine." He sighed into the phone. "I better go find my passport."

The flies were really starting to piss Riley off. She swatted at them and flicked her long braid over her shoulder. With all the horses and animals congregated on Arabella

Plains preparing for today's muster, it was no surprise the flies were swarming. Riley had almost forgotten just how annoying they were, made worse by this never-ending drought.

She waved one persistent fly away from the mare's doleful brown eyes, before lifting the horse's chestnut-coloured leg up and drawing it gently towards her, stretching and smoothing the skin beneath the saddle's girth. After repeating the same exercise with the mare's nearside leg, Riley gave her one last pat, put her foot in the stirrup, and vaulted lightly into the saddle.

Settling in, she surveyed the rugged beauty of the land, feeling a twinge of jealousy at her friend's good fortune. Darcy McGuire and his fiancée, Meghan, had bought a mismanaged property and turned it into a thriving cattle station and horse stud. It was regularly featured in *Outback* magazine and on *ABC Rural*. It hadn't been easy, especially with the drought pushing prices up. But after two years, the couple were finally ready to concentrate on other matters: namely their long-awaited wedding.

Friends since they had met at the local aero club several years ago, Darcy and Riley always made the effort to meet up whenever in the same town, which wasn't often, given Riley's nomadic career. Riley's world was a solitary one of outdoor work and adventures. She never stayed anywhere too long and was constantly meeting new people.

Riley walked the well-behaved mare around the other cowboys and cowgirls who were also tending their horses and preparing for a long day in the saddle. She nodded at the few she recognised from past jobs. She had travelled extensively throughout Western Australia, New South Wales, and the Northern Territory for work over the years, but always enjoyed her time in Queensland. It was her home state and she loved the stoic nature and down-to-earth sense of humour of the locals.

She directed her horse to the tent where the vet nurse was waiting for her.

Bride-to-be Meghan smiled broadly, hands on her hips as Riley approached, her Kelpie dog at her feet. "This isn't your usual mode of transport."

Riley dismounted and patted the mare's neck. "Not a bad way to travel though. She's a beauty."

"This is Shadow." Meghan tickled the horse's hairy nostrils and Shadow blew softly. "She's our best mother but is also great on a muster. Thanks for getting her ready for me."

"No problem." Riley stood aside as Meghan ran her hands over the horse. As the community's vet nurse, it was Meghan's job to ensure all the horses were healthy enough to muster. If an animal became lame on the job it could cost valuable time and manpower.

"She's good to go. I'll keep her here until I'm done."

Riley nodded and bent to pat the dog. "You ready for the muster too, Banjo?"

The dog yipped in reply, his tail sweeping in wide arcs across the dirt floor. Riley missed having a canine companion of her own, and Banjo reminded her of the pup she had been given as a child. Named after her favourite country singer, Cash had died after eating poisonous bait meant for wild, feral dogs. He had only been two years old. Riley hadn't owned another one since. Her career made pet ownership impossible anyway.

She finished patting the dog and checked to make sure no one was waiting to see Meghan. "Everything set for the wedding then?"

Meghan's whole face lit up with her smile. "Yeah I think everything's finally organised. I can't believe it's only a week away. We've been waiting so long for this."

Riley raised an eyebrow. "And is Lachie onboard?"

"He is, thankfully. He's still raw about it. I mean, two years ago I was supposed to marry him and here I am about to marry his brother." Meghan rubbed her neck. "But we both know it wouldn't have worked out. Once I met Darcy, there was never going to be anyone else."

Riley smiled. Darcy had told her the whole sorry saga and how the morning of her wedding to Lachie, Meghan had fled home to Townsville. She had fallen in love with Darcy while engaged to his brother.

Riley only knew Lachie by reputation but doubted he would be much of a match for Darcy with his loyalty and gentle soul. He was the type of man who would have your back no matter what. Riley had never felt anything romantic for him herself, but she could see why Meghan had fallen for him.

"Isn't there another brother too?" Riley vaguely remembered Darcy mentioning him. "Is he coming to the wedding?"

"Noah. He's the youngest." Meghan's eyes brightened. "He's here actually. Just arrived yesterday and surprised us all. We weren't expecting him until the wedding. Anyway, he's been working with horses all his life, so he's joining the muster today. I'll try to introduce you this evening."

Riley smiled. She couldn't help but be a little bit curious about the elusive third McGuire brother. No one ever spoke about Noah—not even Darcy.

A group of riders approached the tent and Riley moved out of their way. "I'll let you get to it. See you tonight."

"Be safe out there," Meghan said.

Riley threw a wave back at Meghan, but her mind was already on the job—*head east and drive out the cattle.* Western Queensland was mostly flat scrub, but cattle liked to find shade and cover under the old gums and coolabah trees. It would be a relatively easy day if all went to plan, although she was the only chopper pilot in the sky today. It wasn't like in the Pilbara where she and Grant had worked for weeks on a muster, getting into canyons and crevasses no man had ever set foot in.

A smile spread across her face as she approached her dark blue Robinson R22, the blades tied down just as she'd left them last night. She ran her hand lovingly over the smooth nose. This was her best friend, her baby. All her savings had gone into flying lessons, then this chopper, and she'd paid for it all herself.

After opening the door, Riley climbed inside, retrieved her clipboard, and started her pre-flight checklist. *Safety first.* Grant's familiar mantra was uppermost in her mind. This job was dangerous enough without taking any unnecessary risks.

A significant number of helicopter mustering pilots in Australia died on the job. In her six years in the business, she had been to more funerals than she cared to remember. But it was a job that called to her and she did it well. Sure, she had scars to show for it, and she'd had a hell of a lot of close calls. But being up in the sky with only a thin shell of metal, a small motor, and two blades keeping you from falling to the hard earth below was a feeling like no other. That was her office, her home, and she couldn't wish for anything better.

After a thorough walk around, testing blades, rudders, fluid, and oil, then releasing the blades, she was good to go. She glanced at her watch. Right on time.

Riley climbed into the small two-seater machine and put her paperwork away before strapping on her seat belt. She depressed the engine-starter button until it fired, and then reached over to push the fuel cut-off. Riley did a final look around and she was ready to fly.

With one hand on the stick, she rolled on the throttle and felt the familiar lift. Excitement and adrenaline flowed through her.

Just another day on the job.

CHAPTER 2

*T*he deep *whop-whop-whop* of a helicopter echoed over the paddocks. Noah's horse shook her head and whinnied from where it stood, waiting for the go ahead for the muster to start.

"Shh, it's okay," he murmured, reaching to stroke her dark brown mane. He twisted in the saddle to watch the dark blue chopper lift off, kicking up dust in its wake. Mustering with helicopters certainly made the job faster. From their aerial vantage, the pilot could spot then move beasts from their tricky hiding spots.

Noah had participated in heli-mustering regularly both at Brigadier Station and also in Otago. The terrain there had been mountainous, and the light-coloured sheep were easily camouflaged in the dense bush. Today they would be mustering Darcy's Droughtmaster beef cattle. And from what Noah had seen, this herd seemed to be in good condition, despite the decade-long drought.

"Ready there, cowboy?"

Noah turned at the familiar voice; Darcy trotted over on his sleek black horse.

"Who are you calling cowboy?" Noah raised his brows. His brother was practically Queensland's version of *The Man from Snowy River*. If anyone was going to ride a horse at full gallop down a steep mountain, it would be Darcy McGuire. Not because he was brave, but because he was skilled and could ride better than anyone else Noah knew.

He had no desire to compete with his brother. Noah had nothing but respect and love for him. Darcy was the reason he had come back. His brother had saved his life more than once when they were kids.

Noah lifted his eyes to the sky. "See you got a helicopter. That must be costing a bit."

Darcy readjusted his Akubra. "That'll save us about two days' work. Worth every penny."

After getting Meghan's tick of approval, the mounted musterers and their cattle dogs took off in various directions, following Darcy's instructions on where the cattle would be found.

"You're with me, mate." Darcy waved Noah over. "We're helping the chopper."

Noah nodded and steered his horse next to his brother and the two Kelpie dogs.

They galloped for a long time over the parched countryside, the sound of the chopper's motor getting louder above them.

Darcy slowed his horse and gestured to Noah to pull up beside him. Noah watched as he tugged out a radio and spoke into it, his words whipped away by the wind. Before Noah could comment, the familiar blue bird rose up from the bush and circled around them. He briefly glimpsed the pilot's khaki shirt before it banked and spun a one-eighty. Both men watched in silent awe as the pilot overshot the clearing and banked the chopper to come back around to the small sandy patch by the river. The tiny machine manoeuvred between scrub, pushing cattle from their shady hiding spots. It hovered mere metres from the dirt before lifting its tail in the air, bringing the blades at an angle that was almost vertical. Noah's heart thudded fast, adrenaline flooding his system at the dangerous stunt.

The chopper moved forward slowly, and Noah held his breath.

The pilot had better know what he was doing.

The manoeuvre worked, and four cattle were pushed out of their hiding place by the noisy machine and into the clearing. Darcy rounded behind them and motioned for Noah to take the left side.

Swallowing, Noah moved into position. He threw the blue machine a final glance. It angled back and lifted off, then dipped and flew away behind them. Noah's heart rate slowly returned to normal as he trotted his horse alongside the cattle, pushing them to the yards.

He couldn't help but replay in his mind the moves the helicopter had made. That pilot was either crazy or very capable to pull off such a dangerous manoeuvre. A hidden power line or stray branch could be the difference between flying and crashing.

The mob was strung out but moving in the right direction. From his position on the wing, he squinted ahead through the heat haze and flies. A group of cattle were working their way to the front. If they managed to bust out of the mob, they would head for the thick band of scrub at the eastern end of the paddock and become nearly impossible to find without calling the chopper to help. He whistled for the closest Kelpie and was impressed when his brother's faithful dog needed little instruction. It found the animals and stalked them into submission.

The return journey was long and by mid-morning, the sun's rays were biting his bare neck and arms. Noah wiped sweat from his forehead, unused to this heat. Otago was freezing cold and snowing in winter, but pleasantly mild in summer. Here in Central Queensland in August, it was already hotter than any weather he had experienced since leaving.

As they came closer to the yards, he saw a large number of cattle were already assembled there; some had already found their way to the troughs and the others were feeding their way towards it, having been pushed by another group of musterers. The mob were still quite spread out, so Darcy sent his dogs wide and followed slowly on his horse. It didn't take long for the cattle to notice the dogs skirting them at a distance, and they began to mob up and start moving again.

Finally, Darcy and Noah reached the holding paddock with adjoining cattle yards, and herded the beasts in before dismounting and resting their horses for lunch.

Hearty homemade pies and sandwiches were laid out on tables under the wide verandah of the main house. Noah joined the line of fellow workers and helped himself to a corned beef and cheese sandwich and fruit.

Taking a seat at an empty table, he took a mouthful of sandwich and gazed out at the landscape so foreign and yet so familiar to him. He let satisfaction at knowing he'd done a good, honest morning of hard work roll over him. Things weren't so bad after all.

He looked up as the deep humming of the helicopter filled the air before it flew overhead, and then slowly lowered to the flattened area where Darcy was waiting. Noah could just make out the pilot's silhouette as he reached and pushed some buttons, powering the bird down before swinging open the door.

Noah put the last of his sandwich in his mouth and almost choked as he watched the pilot climb out and swing long brown hair over her shoulder. He was humbled to admit it, but the thought that the pilot was female hadn't even crossed his mind.

Noah took the opportunity to study her long, denim-clad legs and curvy hips. Her khaki, short-sleeved shirt was tucked in at the waist and cinched with a leather belt. Her slender arms had seen plenty of sun and her face was hidden by a worn Akubra. As she bent to tie down the blades, heat flooded his veins. Hers was a body he wouldn't mind snuggling up to, and he hadn't wanted to snuggle up to a woman in a long time.

Shaking his head, he stood and cleared away his dishes. As he poured himself a cup of hot coffee and tried to dispel the thoughts going through his mind, Darcy called him.

Noah turned too fast and the drink lurched to the lip of his cup, right towards a curvy khaki shirt. Her reflexes were fast though, and she stepped back just in time so the coffee splashed onto the floor instead of her top.

He was left staring at her chest. And what a chest it was.

"Up here, cowboy." The melodic lilt of her voice reminded him of a country singer.

He raised his eyes from full, rounded breasts to her face. His heart skipped a beat as he took in the chocolate brown of her eyes—narrowed and assessing him.

Beside her, Darcy cleared his throat. "Riley, this is my little brother, Noah." His voice was edged with humour. "Noah, this is my old friend and our very skilled helicopter pilot, Riley Sinclair."

Riley put a slender hand out and Noah shook it, surprised by her firm grip. Her features were soft, and sun-bronzed. A strand of long hair was stuck to her cheek and his fingers itched to touch it.

"Nice to meet you," he said, remembering his manners. "Sorry about"—he waved his hand between them—"that."

She shrugged. "Accidents happen." She turned to pour herself a cup, and Noah frowned as Darcy smiled slyly at him before strolling away.

"Darcy said that you just got back from New Zealand." Riley glanced at him as she added milk to her drink.

Noah gulped some coffee before answering, "Yeah, I've been in Otago for the last eight years working on a sheep station." He braced for the inevitable sheep joke that usually followed.

"It's beautiful there. I went skiing in Wanaka last year and had a great time. Their merino wool is the best. I brought a beanie and jersey back with me but haven't had the opportunity to wear them." She gestured up at the blazing sun.

The tension that had filled him eased. "Are you from around here?"

"No, I'm from Longreach, but I work all over the place now." She shrugged as though it was no big deal. "You're here for the wedding?"

He nodded. "Yep, then I'm house-sitting this place while Darcy and Meghan are honeymooning."

"Lucky them, huh? Two weeks in Fiji. Sipping cocktails on the beach."

Noah scratched his chin. "I dunno, think I'd rather spend the time skiing. I'm not really one for lazing around."

Riley faced him with an arched eyebrow and a cheeky grin. "But it's their honeymoon. That's not all they'll be doing."

Noah's face heated and his groin tightened. He watched as her eyes crinkled at the sides. She was obviously enjoying making him squirm.

He cleared his throat. "So that was pretty impressive flying out there. I've never met a female pilot."

She stiffened, the teasing tone gone from her voice. "There are plenty of women pilots. Gender has nothing to do with it."

Shit. Way to go, Noah. Put your foot in it that time. "I didn't mean—"

"I'm a hell of a better pilot than a lot of blokes with licences." She put down her half-empty cup before turning and stomping off.

Noah twisted his face to the sun and swore. He'd

wanted to give her a compliment, but it had all come out wrong. He was out of practise when it came to woman and how to treat them. No wonder Jade had kicked him out.

Riley was the first woman he had been attracted to in a long time. Probably a good thing she had stormed off anyway; he was only here for a few weeks, then he would take his inheritance and head back to Otago.

To what? His ex-girlfriend's family farm that didn't need him anymore. He didn't have any good mates there.

If only he had someone he could share it all with. A partner maybe, someone who could complement his skills. He could do the ground mustering, and she could assist in her chopper and …

His cheeks heated as he swallowed the last of his coffee. What was he thinking?

Around him the tables were being cleared and Riley was nowhere to be seen. Time to get on with the job he was here for and forget about the pretty pilot.

CHAPTER 3

*R*iley shut and locked the helicopter door before turning and leaning against it. She took deep breaths of the dry country air and looked out at the world washed with warm golds, pinks, and browns. The harshness of the dried-out land was softened by the slanting rays of the setting sun. Hidden hues emerged in the landscape that was largely bleached of colour in the full daylight.

Pride at a job well done mingled with the remaining annoyance over Noah's chauvinist comment earlier that day. Of course she had heard worse comments and taunts about female pilots, but it never stopped bothering her. These men didn't know what she had gone through to get here. What she'd had to give up and go without.

She had been a bit harsh though. Noah hadn't deserved her rudeness.

He was certainly a fine-looking man with his broad shoulders and tapered waist. He had cut a nice picture riding his horse today. She wouldn't mind taking him for a ride herself. From the way he had been staring, he was certainly attracted to her. A night with Noah wouldn't be the worst way to spend her free time.

With a sigh, she pushed off the helicopter, swung her bag over her shoulder, and started walking to the homestead. Right now, what she wanted was a shower and hot meal.

The cattle were safely grouped in the yards. Their bellowing was deafening as they called to their lost loved ones. Dust churned up by their hooves floated in the breeze, mingling with the tantalising aroma of barbequed meat.

She followed the directions Darcy had given her to the ringers' quarters. Three fibro demountable buildings arranged in a U-shape.

The bunk room was quiet; the workers who were staying tonight must have already showered and gone to the homestead for a night of banter and booze. Riley found herself a vacant bottom bunk and threw her belongings on it before unzipping her bag and gathering up her toiletries.

The shower stalls and toilets were located in the adjoining demountable and she couldn't help but smile at the deep, rumbling hum coming from one of the shower cubicles. She wondered who it was with such a deep baritone.

Having been warned about the old pipes, she waited patiently for the singer's shower to turn off before putting hers on.

As she waited for the water to warm up, she studied herself in the mirror. Her face was windblown and bronzed from her life outdoors. She never wore make-up, wouldn't know how to put it on even if she had to, and her only skincare regime was smearing sunscreen on after brushing her teeth.

She took out her comb and loosened her long brown plait. Her hair was naturally straight and was always tied up, so she had very few knots to brush out. It occurred to her, as she piled it into a loose bun on top of her head that it was time to get a few inches cut off.

The cubicle door behind her opened and she glanced over as a bare-chested man emerged with a towel wrapped low around his hips. Water dripped from his muscled pecs and he stopped abruptly as their eyes met. Her cheeks burned, and she forced herself to close her mouth.

"Sorry. I didn't hear you come in." Noah backed up as if to retreat into the privacy of the cubical.

Riley gestured to her shower stall. "I was just waiting for the water to heat up. It should be okay now." Though a cold shower could be just the trick right now. She stepped into the stall. As she turned to close the door, she caught Noah's reflection in the mirror. She memorised every inch of bare skin. The fine sprinkling of dark hair across his chest, and the trail that led from his navel downwards below the towel, sent her imagination wild.

She leaned back against the door with her eyes closed. She wasn't sure if Darcy would be too happy with her if she seduced his brother, especially this close to his wedding. Then again, Noah seemed pretty wound up to her. Maybe he needed to release all that pent-up energy.

As she washed, she had to force herself not to give in to the fantasies that were rolling over her.

When she was out and dried off, she dressed in jeans and a red checked shirt then opened the door just enough to peek through. Her shoulders sank slightly with disappointment that he wasn't still there.

After putting away her dirty clothes and toiletries, she made her way up to the homestead. Riley meandered through the crowds of people who had gathered on the verandah to celebrate a job well done.

Her stomach rumbling, she filled her plate with food and found an empty seat with a group of older men—ringers and stockmen with weathered faces and eyes that spoke of years of hard work. Conversation ebbed and flowed as steak burgers and thick, chunky fries were enjoyed while from across the paddocks came the occasional cattle's low. A quad bike revved in the distance; someone out checking the stock. They were the sounds, scents, sights, and atmosphere of a beautiful day in a beautiful land. This was a life loaded with joy and challenge.

As the warmth of camaraderie and shared laughter wrapped themselves around her, Riley relaxed. She enjoyed evenings like this—good company sharing good stories after a good day's work.

"You must have seen a few things," the man on her right said to her. "How long have you been flying?"

People were always interested in learning more about what Riley did and where she had worked. So she happily spoke about her favourite topic and shared some of her best stories with them.

As the conversation shifted to other subjects, Riley found herself searching the crowd for one particular cowboy.

She spotted Noah standing on the far side of the verandah, surrounded by a group of men. His stance was stiff and his expression serious and tense. Was he always like this around a large group of people? Again, her mind travelled to all the ways she could help him relax.

He was wearing a blue shirt which brought out the azure colour of his remarkable eyes. Her heart beat a little bit harder as she remembered that delicious bare chest below it.

She shook away her dirty thoughts. She didn't know the first thing about this guy. He could already be in a relationship—although there had been no mention of one when she had spoken to Meghan that morning. The fact that her friends liked him so much only spoke well of Noah's character. Was he like Darcy? The strong, silent type who, when they gave their heart, gave it forever?

Not that she was looking for that. It was unfair to ask any man to have a relationship with her when she worked away most months of the year. And the chances of her being injured or killed on the job were higher for her than even those in the military. She didn't want to think about all the widows her colleagues had left behind.

She concentrated on finishing her meal in peace. When she returned to Longreach, she would head to the local pub and see if there were any new cowboys in town looking for a fun night.

"Go easy on him."

Riley jumped when Darcy sat next to her.

"What?"

Darcy nodded in his brother's direction. "He's just coming out the back end of a long-term relationship. Turns out the girl he went to New Zealand for broke up with him and has started seeing another bloke right under his nose."

"That's too bad." Riley tried to sound nonchalant but wasn't sure she pulled it off. "How long had they been together?"

"Since high school. Jade was over here on an exchange and when school finished, she took him back with her." Darcy leaned in closer so as not to be overheard. "He said he was in love, but I think it might have just been an excuse to leave home."

"Why would he want to leave so badly? I thought you guys had a great childhood."

Darcy's gaze darkened. "It wasn't all that great. Noah's in particular."

Riley itched with curiosity. She wanted to know more. What had happened? What was Darcy talking about?

But his eyes warned her not to ask him.

"It's great he came back then, for your wedding," she said.

"No one is more surprised or happy about it than me." Darcy grinned. "He's a down-to-earth, fair-dinkum bloke."

"Not like Lachie?"

"Hell no. Jade was Noah's first and only girlfriend. Meghan wants to set him up with someone while he's here. She wants everyone to be happy now, just like us."

Riley watched as Darcy searched for his fiancée in the

crowd, and their eyes locked for a moment. It was enough for even the most sceptical person to believe that true love did exist. And for the first time in her life, Riley's heart ached.

She had never known a marriage that was happy. Her parents had divorced when she was a newborn, and Riley had been raised by her grandmother. Her mother had made an appearance at the occasional Christmas lunch which would inevitably end badly. Yes, Riley knew all about dysfunctional families and their drama.

But she'd had the love and support of her cousin, Grant, who had encouraged her in school to become a pilot like him. By the time she had earnt her pilot's licence, Grant had a few years' experience and had started his own business.

Riley was his first and only employee. They still regularly worked together on musters and other projects requiring multiple helicopters. But, unlike Riley, Grant was more of a homebody and had found happiness with his long-term girlfriend, Andrea. Grant ran the successful business from their home base in Longreach, while Riley spent her time in the sky. It was a partnership that suited them both.

Riley took her plate to the kitchen and had just finished serving up a slice of pavlova for dessert when Meghan called her over.

Too late, Riley realised Noah was sitting at the same table as her friend's fiancée and the only vacant spot on the bench was next to the broad-shouldered hunk of a man. She chewed on her lip as she climbed over the bench. He shuffled over, allowing her an extra inch of space. When she was settled, she felt the heat radiating off him. His hard thigh pressed against hers, tempting her to touch him to see if other parts of his body were also long and hard.

She scooped up a spoonful of the fluffy sweet dessert and shoved it in her mouth before she could worry her lip raw.

"Noah was just about to tell us about working in New Zealand," Meghan said before turning the floor over to him.

Noah shifted in his seat and Riley sensed he didn't like being the centre of attention.

"It's not too different, working with sheep. Except they have to be shorn. That's a skill that takes a fair bit to master."

He was so close she could see the faded freckles across his nose and the faint dimple in his chin. His masculine scent was subtle and fresh, reminding her of rolling green pastures. He lifted a can of Coke to his mouth, and she watched his Adam's apple bob along with the movement before he lowered his drink and twisted to let his gaze slip over hers.

God, she wanted to taste him. The thought slipped recklessly into her mind and her gaze dropped, drawn to his mouth. His lips were just inches away—

Their table companions laughed at a story Meghan was telling, and Riley forced her attention away from Noah and all the things she wanted to do to him.

A gust of cold air replaced his nearness as he climbed out of his seat.

"Another round anyone?" He lifted his empty can to

the group seated around the table and was answered by requests for beers and rums. He raised an eyebrow to Riley who shook her head, reaching for her glass of water instead and quickly slugging it down.

Why was she letting him affect her so much? She normally had better control over her hormones.

Noah soon returned to his seat and after passing out the drinks, he leaned towards her and spoke in a quiet, husky voice. "I'm sorry about earlier. I didn't mean to insinuate that women can't fly. I just meant that I really hadn't met a female pilot before you."

He was so sincere in his apology and he smelled so good, that she couldn't help but forgive him. "Well, to be fair, there aren't many of us. I guess most women have the good sense not to enter into such a dangerous career."

Relief relaxed his jaw and his shoulders lowered. A genuine smile raised sexy to new heights. "Did it affect your training much? Like you had something to prove?"

Her eyes widened. "Yeah, it did." People never asked her about that. But she had worked harder than necessary, not settling for just passing; she'd wanted to ace every test and exam. Even though she wasn't treated any differently from her male counterparts, many of whom were still good friends, she still felt like she had to prove herself every day.

"Well, for what it's worth, I can see why you're so good. Pure determination, strength, and grit. You're one of a kind, Riley Sinclair."

The way he said her name in such a warm, familiar way caused her heart to flutter in her chest. "Thanks." She smothered a self-conscious smile.

He gently nudged her with his shoulder. "You're welcome." He gave her a tender look that liquefied her already molten heart.

She took another sip of water as she tried to compose herself. The men she knew usually only said nice things if they wanted something in return. Even though she wanted that too, she sensed Noah meant what he'd said. Like he would only ever give a compliment if he thought it was genuinely deserved.

"Why did you want to be a pilot?" he asked.

"My cousin, Grant, got me interested in helicopters from a young age. We were always pestering the pilots we knew to take us up and teach us about them."

The curves of Noah's mouth turned up. "You two sound real close."

"He's more like an older brother to me than a cousin. I grew up with our grandmother but spent a lot of time on the station with him and his family. He's a pilot too. Technically he's my boss, but we're more like partners in the business. I get to do the flying, and he gets to do the paperwork."

"No brothers or sisters?"

"Nope, just me." She nodded in Darcy's direction. "What was it like growing up with him?"

Noah's expression darkened. "It was a house full of boys so there was a lot of fighting and arguing." He took a deep swallow of his soft drink, and she got the distinct impression that, just like Darcy, he did not want to talk about his childhood either.

She shifted the conversation to safer ground instead. "Tell me more about New Zealand."

She watched as he relaxed back into the chair and the tension drained from his eyes. "It's really bloody cold."

She laughed at his comment. Western Queensland rarely got below freezing and was mostly stinking hot and humid in summer. For a born-and-bred outback cowboy, New Zealand's temperate climate must have been quite a shock.

"Otago is so far south it gets the Antarctic wind. It can chill you right to the bone. But it sure is a beautiful country."

She recalled the white-capped peaks of The Remarkables, the mountain range near Queenstown where she had learned to ski. Nature never failed to impress Riley, and the region had certainly been extraordinary.

"In spring, the pastures are so green, like emeralds—it almost hurt my eyes the first time I saw it. It's so lush and soft. It doesn't take long for the sheep to fatten up eating that."

"It must make the winter easier to bear, knowing spring's coming?"

He looked directly at her as if she had read his mind. "It does."

"Did you learn how to shear?" While in Queenstown, she had visited a sheep station and seen a sheep-shearing demonstration. The man had bent over the woolly animal and had used the noisy clippers to efficiently and quickly cut away the wool so it stayed together in one piece, stuck together by oily lanolin and fibre. It had been an impressive show. Afterwards, she had chatted to the shearer who had admitted to having almost constant back and shoulder pain from years of hard work. But, like her, he took the bad with the good and continued working on the land because it was what he loved to do.

"I was taught how," Darcy said. "I can do a decent fleece but those boys who have been shearing most of their life have got it down to a fine art. It's fun to watch; they compete to get the best time and the most sheep because they get paid per bale of wool."

Riley, resting her head in her palm, listening intently as Noah regaled her with stories from the shearing shed. He spoke with a passion for the work and lifestyle that she couldn't help but admire.

"There was this one Merino ram that avoided being mustered in for years. When he was finally caught, he had huge, long horns and a filthy thick coat," Noah explained with a chuckle. "The farmer named him Shrek, after the movie. He's become something of a Kiwi legend."

"I think I remember hearing about that." Riley grinned. "It made the news here."

There was a pause in their conversation and Riley looked up to see nothing but empty tables around them.

Noah glanced at his watch. "We must have lost track of time."

Riley stretched her arms above her head and yawned. "We had better get some shut-eye. Another big day tomorrow."

They stood and walked together down the dimly lit path towards their quarters.

"Which one are you in?" Noah asked as they arrived in front of the demountables.

Riley pointed to the one on the left where her bunk was waiting.

"I'm that one." He nodded to the building on the right as he shoved his hands in his pockets.

In the faint light, she could just make out his rugged features. She'd never felt so drawn to a man before, so compelled and fascinated. Everything in her wanted to close the distance between them. But at the same time, the sheer intensity of her need made her hesitate.

An owl hooted noisily and broke the moment. Riley exhaled on a soft laugh and grinned. "I had fun tonight. Thanks."

Disappointment flickered over his face. "Me too. Have a good night."

"Sleep well." She turned and walked the few steps to the door, which creaked as she opened it. Before she stepped inside, she turned to see if Noah was still there.

He was.

With a smile, he raised a hand in a brief wave before moving off towards his own building.

She couldn't help but smile smugly. He wanted her. Just like she wanted him.

If it wasn't for the damn shared accommodation and bunk beds …

CHAPTER 4

*N*oah was paired up with his brother again the next day, and they continued to flush out the cattle and push them into the yards. The truck was due at midday, and Darcy kept glancing at his watch. Time was money, their father had always said. The man had been sparing when it came to anything except his drink.

With the cattle dogs obediently keeping the beasts moving, Darcy sidled up next to Noah. "Remember when we were kids and we used to practice roping?"

Long-forgotten memories emerged of them trying to figure out how to tie a lasso and throwing it around fenceposts. Despite himself, Noah smiled at the memory; there were only a handful of good ones.

"You picked it up quicker than me. I hear you are some big campdrafting star now."

Darcy shrugged. "My campdrafting days are over. Besides, I just spent more time practising. You lost interest in it."

Noah shifted in the saddle. "It wasn't that I lost interest. Dad found me practising one day and told me off for wasting my time. He said that I could never be as good as you and Lachie, so I stopped trying."

Darcy halted his horse abruptly. "He told you that?"

Noah pulled on his reins and turned to his brother. "He said that kind of stuff all the time." *And worse.*

"Shit, I never realised. I really missed doing that with you."

"When you went to boarding school, it was just me, Mum, and Dad rattling around the place. It was hard." Noah forced the words out. Darcy didn't know the truth. What their father, Daniel, had really been like.

Noah could still feel the bruises like it was yesterday. The yelling and his mother's screaming would still wake him at night. "I just couldn't take any more. I couldn't stay, not even for Mum." His eyes stung with emotion.

Darcy faced him, his jaw tense and his eyes filled with apology. "I'm sorry I couldn't do more. Stop him."

Noah nodded slowly. "None of us could. It's not your fault." He nudged his horse back to the mob and continued moving forward. That was what he did now—moved forward. He only glanced back if he had to. He didn't want to remember the pain and suffering he had endured at his father's hand. He had spent ten years trying to get away from Daniel's disappointed looks and hard fists. Even though his father was dead, Noah was scared Daniel's ghost would always haunt him.

Spotting a small group of stray cattle, Noah turned his horse, grateful for a distraction. As he rode slowly towards them, the cattle lifted their heads to watch him warily. He stopped and whistled to the dogs, casting them out wide behind the mob. When they were still a long way out from the cattle, he made them drop. For several minutes, the cows eyed the dogs in the grass and shifted nervously. He whistled again, and the dogs stood and walked slowly towards the cattle who obediently started moving forward. Soon they joined the bigger herd being mustered to the yards.

Noah let the peace and tranquillity of the outback settle over him. The warm sun was nice after the cool alpine winds. The smell of cattle and dust was so different from damp wool and grassy pastures.

Overhead, the faint sounds of spinning rotors whooshed. He turned to watch as the familiar bird circled nearby. Riley held it in a hover over a dense tree line, and he watched as a fat cow trotted towards them, a cattle dog behind it.

For all the bad memories, there were some good ones too. Darcy had reminded him of that. Noah loved this land; it was in his blood. His ancestors had worked this dirt for generations.

All his life, he had let his father control him. Leaving the outback had gotten him away from his father, but he'd also had to give up his rightful inheritance. With his father gone, maybe he could finally come back and live the life he wanted. Maybe his future was here. At twenty-eight, he still wasn't entirely sure what he wanted to do or where his future lay. It was a scary thought, but kind of exciting too.

He watched the helicopter fly away into the horizon and imagined Riley at the controls. He had never met anyone like her before—so headstrong and smart. He ached just thinking about her in her tight shirt and aviator sunglasses. *Shit.* He wanted to touch her, to feel those soft curves under his palms. To smell her hair and stroke her cheek. She stirred deep emotions in him that had long been suppressed.

Darcy sent out a loud whistle, and Noah turned his thoughts back to the job at hand. They were almost at the yards, and right on time. The cattle truck was just pulling up.

Many hands made light work. The cattle were sorted and loaded quickly and efficiently. As the sun started its slow journey towards the western horizon, the men and women began leaving the station, heading for their homes or next jobs.

Noah had searched the quarters for Riley. He'd wanted to see her one more time before she left. To see if there really was something between them.

Disappointment settled uncomfortably in his stomach as he trudged up the stairs to the homestead.

Chatter filtered through the open window as he removed his boots. He glanced inside to see Riley, her earth-brown hair hung loose over her shoulders. She laughed at something Meghan said, and it was the most beautiful sound he had ever heard.

After opening the door with determination, he entered the room. "Evening."

Meghan and Riley both turned to him but before either could say anything, another woman caught his eye.

"Hello, son."

"Mum."

Her face was more lined than he remembered and her hair was now as white as snow.

"What are you doing here?"

Harriet McGuire stood a full foot shorter than him, but he still felt small in her presence. Like a child again.

"I couldn't wait to see you. We weren't expecting you until the wedding." Tears filled her eyes, and shame washed over Noah. He had seen her cry more often than he cared to remember, but he had never been the cause of those tears.

She went to him and he allowed her to wrap her arms around him.

When she finally stepped back, her eyes were glistening. "I've missed you," she said.

Feelings he had kept buried so deep for so many years bubbled to the surface. There had been bad times, but there had also been good ones. He still loved his mother and knew he always would.

Gently, he wiped a tear from her cheek. "I missed you too, Mum."

The family settled at the table as Meghan and Harriet laid out plates of roast potatoes, parsnips, and pumpkin. Carved roast beef with gravy was passed around, and Noah helped himself to the succulent meat.

They fell into easy conversation with talk of the muster. Riley carried on a lively discussion with Meghan, the two women laughing as though they'd always been best friends. Riley fitted into their family seamlessly. He could see why Darcy had liked her. Darcy chose friends cautiously after all, making sure to establish a strong foundation of trust and honesty before he truly called anyone friend.

Apart from being beautiful and smart, Riley was funny and compassionate too—qualities Noah found equally attractive in a woman.

From the corner of his eye, Noah noticed his mother watching him. She tilted her head and raised her eyebrows questioningly in Riley's direction.

Noah lowered his gaze and concentrated on his food, hoping his mother hadn't seen the glimmer of desire in his eyes.

"So, Mum," Darcy said, "how are things on Brigadier Station?"

Harriet put down her utensils. "Not too bad. Although Lachie is understaffed at the moment."

Noah watched as both his brother and soon-to-be sister-in-law shared a knowing glance. Lachie wasn't the easiest man to get on with at the best of times. And according to Darcy, he was drinking more than he should. Spending the precious money that Brigadier Station earned on booze and entertainment.

Harriet looked across the table at Noah. "Now that the muster is over, I wondered if you could come back with me? Help your brother out?"

"That wasn't part of the deal." Noah breathed out.

"I know. I'm sorry. Forget I asked." Harriet's shoulders slumped.

Noah speared a chunk of meat with his fork, put it in his mouth, and chewed.

"You're always welcome to stay here," Meghan said to him before turning to Riley. "What are your plans now?"

"I've got a job working for Dylan Sears. Do you know him?"

Noah looked up at the familiar name while Harriet clapped her hands together. "Dylan and Maddie are our neighbours. Oh, I'm glad he's hired help. He's been a bit off lately and needs an extra set of hands."

"Darcy got me the job. It's just until the wedding," Riley replied.

As Harriet told Riley all about Dylan and his young family, Noah glanced between the two women. Suddenly, there was no reason to stay at Arabella Plains when he was needed at Brigadier Station.

Riley being so close certainly sweetened the deal. It wouldn't be so bad, living under the same roof as Harriet and Lachie if it meant he might run into Riley in town.

He would just need to spend the night preparing for the altercation that was sure to come when he saw his eldest brother again.

"So, Mum," he said, "what time are we leaving tomorrow?"

Noah was cleaning dishes at the kitchen sink when he sensed he was being watched. Turning, he saw Riley leaning against the doorframe, her slender denim-clad legs crossed at the ankle.

"Need a hand?"

He reached for the dishtowel and tossed it to her. "Thanks."

She stood next to him, drying pots in silence. He fumbled for something to say, berating himself for feeling so nervous around her. She was just so damn beautiful, it was intimidating. Did she even know the way he reacted to her?

"I hope you don't mind that I'll be working at Dylan's place," Riley said.

"No, of course I don't mind." He turned to look fully at her. She stood within arm's reach, and he itched to touch her.

"You just acted a bit weird at dinner." She reached around him to place a pot on the table and he caught a whiff of her fruity shampoo.

"That wasn't because of you. I haven't been back in many years. I'm a bit nervous about it."

She studied him for a moment. "It must have been terrible."

"What?"

"Whatever made you run away." She placed her hand on his arm. "You don't have to tell me if you don't want to, but I'm here if you need me."

He gulped. "Thanks."

She smiled and squeezed his arm before turning back to the dishes.

He watched her long shiny hair swish behind her as she moved.

He had never told anyone what his father had done. The kind of person he truly had been. Yet he sensed Riley understood somehow. Not even Jade had suspected the truth of his past, and they had been together for almost a decade.

Riley managed to exude truth and honesty with everything she said and did. And because of it, he wanted to tell her all about his rough childhood: his cruel father and seemingly perfect oldest brother. He wanted her to know him. The real him. But he worried that if she saw that side of him—weak and powerless—she might not like it.

CHAPTER 5

*T*he crooning melody of country music filled the cab of the Land Cruiser as Harriet drove Noah along the straight, sunburnt road towards Julia Creek.

The dusty brown countryside was a far cry from the lush green pastures he had left behind. No longer did fat cattle roam these once fertile lands. Instead the paddocks lay bare, the cattle having been moved south or sold off.

As they drove through town, Harriet pointed out the changes. The old feed barn was still there, as was the pub. No small town was complete without an obligatory watering hole. But the milk bar was gone and Mr Miller's toy store.

Empty shops lined the once-thriving main street and Noah wished there was something he could do. The stark reality was that what affected the farms affected the town and local economy. If the farmers suffered, so did the town. Darcy had told him of several places that had been totally abandoned because of the drought and the current low cattle prices. The workers and stockmen had been forced to move for job security and financial stability.

They continued the long drive, chatting about safe topics such as the upcoming wedding. Harriet truly was fond of Meghan, and it cheered him to see his mother happy.

The shuddering of the Land Cruiser as they drove over the cattle grids signalled the start of the station boundary. Noah swallowed hard as the homestead came into view. It was the house of his childhood. Where he and his older brothers had been raised.

This was the place where he had learned to ride and rope. Where he had constantly tried and failed to please his father. He attempted to bury the painful memories, but reminders were everywhere. That spot in the garden, where his father had beat him for not weeding correctly. That tree where he had used to run and hide, sobbing away his shame in private.

"I don't see Lachie's ute. He must have gone out." Harriet turned the engine off and opened her door.

Noah sat in the passenger seat, taking deep breaths, preparing himself for the ghosts he was sure would be waiting inside for him. Harriet looked at him questioningly.

With nimble fingers, he opened the car door and climbed out of the vehicle then reached in the back and pulled out his bag. Dogs barked and rattled the doors of their cages. The warm spring air smelled of eucalypt, and he raised his eyes as cockatoos screeched in the trees overhead.

After removing his boots at the door, Noah followed

his mother into the kitchen. The room was still the same as it had been the day he had left. Even the dinner plates stacked on the drying rack, the ones with the green rims, were the same ones he had eaten off as a child.

Harriet waved him down the hall. "There are fresh sheets on your bed, but I never changed anything else."

He walked slowly towards his room; the wallpaper and carpet were still the same. A little bit more faded than he remembered, but the same nonetheless. He glanced into the rooms as he passed; just as he remembered them.

Harriet waited outside his door as he passed her, then he stood in stunned silence as he took in the room. On his dresser sat the book he had been reading those last holidays; he'd never finished it. He sat on his single bed and let it take his weight. It was soft, just as he remembered; the mattress had been bought with the bed when he outgrew his cot.

Funny how the room was so familiar and yet so strange. He had never decorated it with posters or pictures. His father would have beaten him if he'd put holes in the walls. Besides, he had known he couldn't stay long-term. He had always planned to leave as soon as possible. Now he was finally back, and his father was gone.

"You really didn't change anything," Noah murmured to his mother, who still stood at the door.

"This will always be your home, Noah."

He stared around the room. Home. What did that even mean?

"I'll put the kettle on," Harriet said and started back up the hall.

Noah unpacked a few things, and then went to explore the rest of the house.

There were some changes. His father's possessions were gone, replaced by ornaments more to Harriet's taste. The family photographs still lined the wall in the living room, and he gazed at them. Dad only appeared in one photo—at their wedding. Noah studied it. Had she known the man she was marrying? How could she have loved such an abusive person?

In the picture they both looked so happy and young. Optimistic about their future, as if it was bright and full of opportunities.

"Would you like a cup of tea, dear?" Harriet called from the kitchen, and he went to join her. He perched himself on the stool as she rifled through Tupperware containers.

She placed a plate of chocolate chip biscuits in front of him before preparing two cups of tea.

"Are these your famous biscuits?" he asked, already knowing from the smell that they were.

She sent him a proud smile. "They were always your favourite."

He bit into the soft centre, and chocolate oozed into his mouth. He moaned appreciatively. The woman could cook.

Harriet placed a mug of tea in front of him and then put her hands on her hips. "What should I make for dinner? We could have steak. Would you like that?"

Noah shrugged noncommittally.

"How about a roast? I have a nice cut of beef in the

freezer. It's not New Zealand lamb, but I'm sure it will be good."

"Don't go to any trouble, Mum." He sipped his tea. "Steak will be fine. I can cook it on the barbeque if you like."

She smiled. "That would be lovely."

They drank in silence for a moment. "Are there any horses left?" Noah asked.

Harriet shook her head. "Darcy took them with him back to Arabella Plains. They were his, after all."

Noah looked up and frowned. "What about Feather?"

Harriet lowered her gaze. "Daniel got rid of Feather after you left."

"Got rid of him? Did he get sold? Do you know who bought him?" Noah had often thought about his beloved quarter horse. Feather had been his. The only thing he had never had to share, not even with his brothers. He had ridden Feather at a few rodeos and had spent hours training him, much to his father's disgust. Noah had found a certain sort of therapy from spending time with his equine friend.

Harriet bit her lip, all the time avoiding her son's gaze. "I'm sorry, Noah. There was nothing I could do."

"What do you mean, Mum?" His pulse throbbed through his veins.

"After you left, he took the rifle out there. We never saw Feather again," Harriet explained.

Noah imagined his beautiful animal decomposing under the harsh sun. Wild animals and birds feasting on his body. He pushed up noisily from the table and raked his hands through his hair. "Bastard," he muttered. "He can burn in hell." Noah stormed out of the room, and the screen door banged noisily behind him. He'd learned to shut down his emotions to survive and to insulate himself from hurt. But even in death, his father had reduced him to that teenage boy again.

He pulled on his boots and walked as fast as he could, not caring where. He jumped gates and fences as he went. He walked and walked until his legs grew tired.

When he finally looked up, he had to take a moment to figure out where he was. Noting the tall gum tree, he realised he was at the edge of the property and that this was their boundary fence.

There were no animals on either side of the long fence line. Noah shielded his eyes against the lowering sun; Dylan's paddocks were even more barren and dry than their own.

A few kilometres from where he stood was Riley. Just thinking about her eased his troubled mind and reminded him of all the good things left in the world.

He savoured the peace that thinking of her evoked in him, focusing on remembering every detail of her beautiful face. Her lightly freckled cheeks, her sparkling eyes. His heart ached to see her again.

He turned back to Brigadier Station and sucked in a deep breath, letting the earthy country smells seep into his body.

His father couldn't control him anymore. He would not let him have that kind of power over his life. "I don't know what happened to make you hate me so much," he said to his father's ghost, "but you can't hurt me anymore."

A warm breeze sent dust lifting past him, taking his words and spreading them far.

Noah looked out over the land, really seeing it for what it was. A land that could make or break a person, a family. It could nourish and provide, but also ruin and cause despair. It was his home. This was where his roots were. Where his ancestors' bones were buried. Their sweat and tears were in every clump of dirt.

He wiped his shirtsleeve across his sweaty forehead before setting off to walk back to the house. He would apologise to his mother for his outburst and also for staying away. It was time to put the past behind them.

It was time he said goodbye to his father.

Noah's mouth watered at the smell of sizzling meat grilling on the barbecue. He could get used to these wholesome home-cooked meals. His pace quickened as he followed the smoke to the verandah but froze as he approached the barbeque.

So like their father with his strong physique, broad shoulders, and sun-bleached hair, Lachlan McGuire had always been popular. The type of man men wanted to be friends with, and women wanted to sleep with.

Lachie stepped back from the barbecue and took a slug from the beer bottle he was holding in his left hand. Again, Noah was struck by how similar his brother was to their father: rarely without a drink in hand. Like father, like son, it seemed. Noah steeled himself as Lachie turned towards him.

His brother's expression was grim. Noah hadn't expected a happy reunion.

"Mum said you were here," Lachie said.

Noah knew how to tread lightly, to avoid saying anything that might provoke a fight. "It's good to see you, Lachie."

Again, Lachie chugged from the bottle, this time draining the remains of the amber liquid. Noah winced as he watched him. How many would he go through before the night was over?

Lachie sized his brother up, and Noah bristled.

"How long are you staying?"

"I'll just be here for a few days, until the wedding, then I'll be looking after Darcy's place while they're away."

Lachie nodded and turned back to the barbecue, dismissing his little brother. Noah breathed out a sigh of relief as he walked away.

When he opened the door, his brother called out to him.

"It's good of you to come back," Lachie said tightly, as though forcing the words out. "I'm sure Darcy really appreciates it. Mum too."

Noah gave his brother a tight smile before walking quickly inside. Maybe Lachie wasn't so like their father after all.

He set the dining table for the three of them and helped his mother bring the food from the kitchen. Lachie placed the steaks down before fetching himself a fresh bottle of beer and sitting opposite his brother.

Harriet sat between her sons. "Noah, do you want a drink?"

He motioned to his glass of water. "I'm fine. Thanks, Mum."

He rarely drank. He'd tried very hard to be nothing like Daniel. Where many abused children grew up to be abusive, Noah had worked diligently to find strategies for dealing with his anger. Now, when provoked and under pressure, he would walk away. He would prefer to be called a coward any day than to cause the sort of pain that had been inflicted upon him.

For several minutes, the only sound at the table was the cutlery clinking against plates. Noah enjoyed every mouthful of the tender station-bred beef. Pride swelled through him at the thought that his family was a part of Australia's agricultural business. Without farmers, suburban people wouldn't be able to so easily buy Australian-grown meat and feed themselves. Without families like his, Australia would suffer.

Lachie set his knife and fork down before taking a drink of beer. Harriet sent him a worried look.

"What happened to that girlfriend of yours? Are you two still together?" Lachie asked.

Noah swallowed his food and took a sip of his water. "No. Jade and I broke up a few months ago."

"So, will you go back to the sheep when you finish here?"

Noah recognised the tone in his brother's voice. It was the same as the one in Daniel's. They'd always been like dogs with a bone, trying to get a reaction from Noah. Trying to start a fight.

Noah shrugged. "Probably, but nothing's set in stone." He glanced at his mother. There was a glimmer of hope in her eyes. Time to change the subject. "Meghan seems to have settled in well to outback life."

"She's a country girl at heart." Harriet smiled fondly. The affection between the two women had been obvious the night before. Meghan was the daughter Harriet had never had. "They work so well together at the station. They have big plans for that place."

Lachie grunted, and Noah turned to him. "I was sorry to hear what happened."

Meghan had dodged a bullet when she had jilted Lachie. She was much safer with Darcy. He would give his life to protect the people he loved from harm.

From all accounts, Lachie was still the selfish, arrogant man he had always been. A man who would constantly put himself first, no matter what it cost anyone else.

"That's all in the past," Lachie said as he stood and went to retrieve another bottle. Noah caught his mother's eye as Lachie cracked it open.

Noah and Harriet had always been good at communicating without speaking. Their simplest observations had sent Daniel into full-on fits of anger. Noah didn't want to see if Lachie was so easily provoked, especially not tonight: their first evening meal together. Over the next few days, he expected Lachie's temper would eventually boil over. He would have to prepare himself and be ready for it.

Lachie sat back in his chair and belched loudly. "I've gotta go to the Isa tomorrow. There's a new shipment of quad bikes arriving."

Harriet sat up a little bit straighter and folded her

hands in her lap. "Really? After what happened, you want another quad bike?

Noah looked between the two.

Lachie's eyes grew dark. "Yes, Mum, I want another bike. We need one."

Tense moments passed before Harriet stood and stormed from the room.

Noah looked at his brother. "What's wrong with the quad bike you already have?"

"It got totalled a while back. I crashed it into a tree. So, I need a replacement. I'm sick of driving my ute around all the time."

Noah nodded. It made perfect sense to have a quad bike for station use, but he could understand his mother's reason for not wanting harm to befall her son. Deciding not to interfere, he kept his mouth shut.

When Noah didn't say anything more, Lachie stood and pushed out his chair. "I've got work to do," he said as he grabbed his beer bottle.

Noah waited a beat before clearing the table and carrying the dishes into the kitchen where his mother was busily washing up.

He started putting things away. "Do you want to tell me what that was about?"

Harriet's shoulders slumped. "There was an accident. It happened the night Lachie found out Darcy and Meghan were seeing each other. Lachie was drunk and angry and drove off on his quad bike. It was dark, and he crashed into the old gum tree next to the ringers' quarters. The stupid idiot almost killed himself. Darcy and I stayed with him while we waited for the Flying Doctor."

"Shit," Noah muttered under his breath. "That must have been hard for you."

"A mother should never have to go through something like that. We thought he was going to die. I still can't believe he survived it." Tears glistened in her eyes, and he pulled her in for a hug.

"He's a grown man, though, and he'll do what he wants. God knows he doesn't listen to me." She turned her attention back to the dishes.

"And he still likes his beer. He went through quite a few tonight."

"Sometimes he stops. He might go a whole week without a drink, but he always starts back up again. He won't listen to anyone, and he won't get help."

Noah nodded; this was a path he and his mother had been down before.

"I'm sorry you have to go through it again." Emotion swelled in him. "I'm sorry I couldn't protect you from Dad."

Harriet stepped closer to him and wrapped her arms around him. He buried his face into her neck.

"Oh, sweetheart, it wasn't your job to protect me. I was supposed to protect you and I couldn't. I'm sorry." Her voice broke as her tears started. "I wasn't strong enough. I know now I should have left him. I should never have let you go through all of that. I'm so sorry I let you down."

Noah held his mother tightly as he mourned the past. "It's over now, Mum," he said. "We don't have to be victims anymore."

CHAPTER 6

*N*oah easily slipped into the day to day routine at Brigadier Station. With Lachie in Mt Isa, Noah didn't have to worry about bumping into him or reporting back on the jobs he was doing around the property. Instead he just got to work doing the jobs he found which had been neglected too long.

He rediscovered the station, driving Harriet's Land Cruiser through the empty paddocks, checking bores, feeders, and troughs. The station was purposely under-stocked, the majority of the breeders having been moved to agistment in greener pastures down south. Until outback Queensland had a decent wet season, there was nothing for the animals to graze on and it was costly to continually feed the cattle cottonseed.

The Land Cruiser bumped over the uneven terrain and, not for the first time, Noah wished Darcy had left at least one horse in the stable. No wonder Lachie wanted a new quad bike. Despite his mother's fears, he had to agree with his brother. Bikes made more sense than utes or horses in this barren land.

He turned the engine off near the old dam at the edge of the property. Climbing out of the air conditioning, he let the sun beat warmly upon his face. The smell of eucalypt and cow manure brought back memories of swimming and camping out here with his brothers.

He followed the well-worn path down to the dam and stopped to take it all in. Above him, a kookaburra laughed, scaring a kangaroo out of the bush opposite. He smiled at the quintessential Australian bush surrounding him.

Treading carefully, he wandered around the banks of the murky waterhole. He and Darcy had often camped out here to avoid their father. They would bring their swags and cook sausages over an open fire. Darcy would tell him stories, and they would dream about the future.

One day he'd bring his own children here.

Whoa! Where did that come from? He had already made the decision not to have children. Nothing had changed. He would not risk the possibility of being like his father. Of being responsible for screwing up another life in the way Daniel had screwed his up.

No, children weren't in his future, but he might enjoy being an uncle if Darcy and Meghan had kids. Surely they would; they had so much love to give a child, and they would be fantastic role models.

Though Noah tried to focus it elsewhere, his mind kept drifting back to a certain pilot. Did Riley want kids? She didn't seem like the type of woman who would be happy staying at home raising children. Of course, there was nothing wrong with that, but many of his generation were pursuing other dreams and careers, choosing to delay parenthood or not settling down at all.

Before he could think more on the subject, the satellite phone in his back pocket rang.

"When you head into town today, would you be able to pick up the grocery order?" Harriet asked on the other end.

"Sure." In the few days he had been there, Noah had been working on a list of supplies they were short on. He didn't want to step on his brother's toes, but if he was going to fix the tractor as Lachie had asked, he needed to pick up some new parts. "Any idea when Lachie will be back?"

His mother sighed. "Your guess is as good as mine."

Noah brushed his hand over the thick trunk of a gum tree. Lachie had been given this station for no reason other than being firstborn. It was his job to look after it and maintain it for future generations. But Noah got the feeling that Lachie didn't understand what a special gift he had.

Darcy understood. He had stayed on, doing the tough work until he and Meghan had bought Arabella Plains. But it seemed Lachie had let things slip since then.

"No worries, Mum." Noah spoke into the phone. "That's what I'm here for."

The feed store was a hive of activity when Riley pulled up in the farm ute she had borrowed from her employers. Dylan and Maddy Sears were a young couple doing their best on a struggling station, destocked to the point of almost ruin. Riley couldn't help but feel for the weary couple and their young children. She knew they could barely afford her wage, having already laid off their governess and farmhand, but they desperately needed an extra set of hands.

Dylan had made the unusual decision to farm merino sheep, just as first pioneers to the region had. Riley commended his entrepreneurial thinking, experimenting with alternative farming methods, but he had confided to Riley that his ambitious plan wasn't working out as well as he had hoped. Especially since the beef prices had finally started to rise.

Riley climbed out of the ute and made her way into the busy store. She meandered around the aisles, waiting for her order, taking in the products both familiar and new. She was enjoying her time as a hired hand living on the land with regular hours and meals. She also enjoyed playing with Maddie's two children: Jamie, their pre-schooler who toddled around the house getting into all sorts of mischief, and his older sister, Emma, who, when not on the computer doing schoolwork, was helping Maddie with the daily jobs and tending to the animals.

Riley loved watching them interact with each other and laugh at jokes. It reminded her of how little family she had left, and she missed Grant even more.

When Riley's order was ready, she backed the ute up into the loading bay and released the tray.

"Do you need a hand?"

Riley froze. She would know that voice anywhere. It was the voice that filled her dreams at night.

She turned her head, realising her body was in mid-bend and he was getting a very nice view of her rear. The lift at the corners of his mouth proved he had been looking. She straightened and pulled down on her shirt, which had ridden up, exposing pale skin.

"I got this," she said. "Just because I'm a girl doesn't mean I can't lift heavy things."

Noah pushed his Akubra back off his forehead and scratched at his scalp. "I know you can manage it. But I've got a big order coming so I was hoping if I help you then you might just help me."

She grinned and when he returned it with one of his own, she was taken aback at how it changed his face. It was as though pure amusement beamed from every crevice of his skin.

"Well, I guess that's a fair trade then." She nodded and gestured to the pile of lucerne next to her.

They made easy conversation, discussing Dylan's property, the sheep, and the work they were both doing, before speculating over the weather forecast.

"They always say there will be a wet season." Noah stretched his arms high over his head when they had finished her load. "But it's been a long dry spell."

It had been a dry spell for Riley too. Her eyes roamed over Noah's fine physique. Her skin goose bumped, little dimples of exhilaration extending across her arms and shoulders, creeping to her chest.

"Come on, lazybones. You can help me with mine now." Noah nodded over to his waiting Land Cruiser and the barrels of feed and farm equipment waiting to be loaded.

"Are you sure all that's gonna fit?" she asked doubtfully.

"Well, if it doesn't, maybe we can put some in your ute?" He winked at her then, and she clamped her mouth shut as the urge to giggle like a schoolgirl rose in her. How could something as simple as a wink make her turn to jelly?

Riley moved to jump off the back of the tray, when Noah held out his hand to help her down. Ordinarily she would wave a gesture like that away, but the desire to touch him was just too great.

As soon as their skin met, she regretted it. His rough, calloused hand was warm and comforting. She turned to him, their hands still touching, their eyes lingering on each other. Desire and attraction sparked between them and her heartbeat pounded in her ears. Involuntarily she swallowed and watched as his gaze slid down her neck.

She took a step back, pulling her hand free. "Come on. I get paid by the hour."

It took several minutes to squeeze most of Noah's order into the Land Cruiser. A barrel of feed just wouldn't fit, so they rolled that onto Riley's ute before tying it down. She leaned against the tray and took a swig of water from a bottle before offering it to Noah.

"Thanks." As the bottle changed hands, their fingers touched, sending shivers through her arm. She watched as he placed his mouth where hers had just been and drank.

As he lowered it, he raised his other hand and wiped the back of his palm across his mouth. His full lips were surrounded by a days' growth of stubble, giving him a rough, edgy appeal.

He handed the bottle back. This time, she took care not to touch him. The ache in her was so great that she knew if she touched him again, she wouldn't be able to stop.

"Meet you at my house," he said.

She gulped and nodded. "I'll follow you."

"Okay then." He stepped close and brushed a stray strand of hair behind her ear. Her eyes widened, and hope glimmered across his expression before he turned to his vehicle.

Riley spent the entire trip watching the back of the Land Cruiser, thinking about all the delicious and dirty things she wanted to do to Noah McGuire. By the time they turned into the driveway of Brigadier Station, she was a jumble of heat and wanton desire.

They parked in front of the shed and were greeted by the yapping of work dogs. She climbed out and set to work helping Noah unload, hoping the physical exertion would dampen her lusty thoughts.

As Riley was bolting the tray back in place, Harriet approached from the house. The tension between mother and son had been obvious last time she'd been with them, and Riley wondered if they had resolved their issues yet. Harriet was a gracious, caring woman, whose love for her children was obvious in the way she talked about them and looked at them. Riley would have done anything to have had a mother who cared about her. Did Noah realise how lucky he was?

Harriet's voice was bright and cheerful when she greeted her. "Hello, Riley, how lovely to see you again."

"I ran into your son at the feed store," Riley explained,

as Noah walked over from his ute. "Seems he bought more than he could handle."

Harriet grinned. "Well, it was lucky you were there. Come in for smoko. I've made my famous Anzac biscuits."

As though in response, Riley's stomach rumbled loudly. She glanced at her watch warily. There was still so much to do.

"Come on." Noah shifted beside her. "We can't let you leave on an empty stomach."

"Okay, just a quick one," Riley said before falling into step next to Noah and walking towards the homestead.

The wooden floorboards creaked as she stepped inside. Riley couldn't help admiring the house. It had a welcoming, warm feel to it. There were photos on the walls and family treasures on display.

"Noah, take Riley out to the verandah. It's nice there at this time of the day. I'll bring the tea out when the jug's boiled."

Noah nodded and led her through the double doors where a wide verandah gave them a beautiful view of the outlying countryside.

"Wow," she murmured as she took it in. Brilliant blue sky formed a backdrop for sweeping paddocks as far as she could see. The land was flat and brown, broken up only by the occasional gum tree or water tank. It was the familiar Australian landscape that she knew and loved, very similar to the outback around Longreach.

"It is a nice spot," Noah agreed as he sat in a chair and motioned to one next to him.

She sat and inhaled a deep draught of the clean country air. "It must've been amazing growing up here." He stiffened beside her. He had already suggested that his childhood had not been all sunshine and roses. "I'm sorry. I shouldn't have said that."

Noah moved forward and leaned his elbows on his knees, clasping his hands together. He gazed out towards the paddocks, seemingly lost in thought.

Riley reached her hand across and gently touched his knee. Noah turned to look at it curiously before placing his own hand on top of hers. Their gazes met, the air between them electric with anticipation.

"Here we go then." Harriet stepped out onto the verandah carrying a tray of mugs and biscuits. Riley pulled her hand away, hoping Harriet hadn't seen it.

Over smoko, they chatted about the upcoming wedding and Arabella Plains.

"Darcy and Meghan have done wonders with that place." Harriet's voice was full of pride at her son's success both in work and choice of partner.

"They certainly are happy. They make such a great couple," Riley agreed, chewing her third Anzac biscuit.

"My only wish now," Harriet said softly, "is that my other two sons find happiness."

Riley swallowed.

Happiness.

She couldn't help but wonder if that was what she had now. She had a successful career that she enjoyed. Would she be happier if she had a man who loved her and who she loved in return?

She snuck a peek at Noah before realising his eyes were on her too.

"I better go." She stood, her knee knocking the table, making the cups rattle together. "Sorry."

Harriet and Noah also stood.

"You should come over for dinner one night," Harriet said. "Invite Dylan, Maddie, and the kids too. We haven't seen them in such a long time."

"I'll tell Maddie," Riley said, as Harriet enveloped her in a warm, motherly hug.

"Thanks for smoko," Riley said, then scurried to the door and retrieved her boots.

She had just reached the ute when someone stopped her with a hold on her elbow. She spun around quickly, and Noah caught her with his spare hand. "Riley?"

She looked up questioningly at him. "Yes?"

Noah's mouth moved but nothing came out. Anguish twisted his face.

Riley raised herself onto tiptoes and gently kissed his rough cheek. He smelled of dust and sweat, and her heart beat faster. God, she wanted to taste him. To run her hands over the hard edges of his body.

"I'll see you later." Riley conjured up every bit of strength she had in her, climbing into the ute before she did or said something stupid. He didn't stop her as she shut the door and gunned the engine.

She needed to be more careful with Noah. He was the sort of man who, if she wasn't careful, could steal her heart.

CHAPTER 7

The Julia Creek pub still held the familiar scent of spilt beer and cigarette smoke.

Noah had come here often as a teenager. Not to drink and have a good time, but to collect his comatose father after a big night out.

But tonight was not about him.

With only two days left before the big day, Darcy had invited his friends to town for his buck's night.

Lachie had returned from Mt Isa just after midday, and Noah had made a point to stay out of his way until it was time to leave. Lachie had blasted the music in the car so there had been no chance for conversation. Which suited Noah just fine.

He followed his brother through the front door and into the packed main bar. Noah watched as Lachie was slapped on the back and greeted by several of the men sitting around tables, huge mugs of beer in their hands.

Spotting their brother, Lachie and Noah headed to the

bar where Darcy greeted them and introduced them to his friends.

"Thanks for coming." Darcy raised his glass in their direction.

"It's your buck's night; of course I'd come," Lachie said as he slapped his brother's arm. "Now excuse me while I get a beer." Lachie gave Darcy a wink before nudging his way to the bar.

Darcy turned to Noah with a questioning gaze. "How are you two getting on?"

Noah blew out a breath he hadn't realised he was holding. "We haven't killed each other yet, so not too bad considering. He only just got back from Mt Isa today, I had a couple of days of peace without him there."

"Mt Isa? What was he doing up there?"

Noah snuck a look at his brother who was busy chatting up the female bartender. "He went to check out a new quad bike."

Darcy's eyes darkened. "How did he go?"

"It's getting delivered next week."

Darcy took a long, thoughtful swig from his beer, then gestured to Noah's empty hands. "Sorry, mate, you want a drink?"

Noah shook his head. "I'll grab a Coke in a minute. I volunteered to be the designated driver tonight."

"Good on you."

Noah was quickly swept up in interesting conversation with Darcy's friends. They were all men of around the same age and background. Many of their names, if not their faces, were familiar.

He drank his Coke and picked at the chicken wings,

potato wedges, and sausage rolls that were passed around. He was just about to stifle a yawn when the hairs on the back of his neck bristled.

He knew it was her before he saw her approaching. With her wind-tousled hair and dressed in faded work clothes, he'd never seen her look more beautiful.

Their gazes met and she smiled at him, eyes soft and lovely, flipping his heart over.

Noah stood and offered her his seat. She accepted it gratefully. "Sorry I'm late," she said.

He lingered next to her, close enough that he could smell the citrusy scent of her shampoo. "Big day?"

She nodded slowly, looking only at him, as though they were alone and not in a noisy pub surrounded with cowboys. "How about you? Everything okay at Brigadier Station?"

"Yeah, fine," he said, not wanting to talk about himself. He was far more interested in learning more about her. "How are things at Dylan's?" he asked, because it was safer than saying the things he really wanted to say.

She opened her mouth to answer, a crease forming between her brows, but then Darcy was there, thanking her for coming.

Noah took the opportunity to get her a drink from the bar. When he returned, there was a spare seat next to her which he quickly claimed, not wanting to miss the opportunity to spend more time with her. In just a few days, she would go back to her regular life and he might never see her again. The thought frightened him more than he expected.

He watched as she hungrily devoured a chicken wing.

She wasn't dainty about it; she held onto it with her fingers and let the barbeque sauce colour her mouth.

She was something else, alright. He liked that about her. Hell, who was he kidding? He liked everything about her, from her sassy mouth and her ballsy attitude, to her sexy body.

When her tongue whipped out to lick some juice, he felt his jeans tighten.

"I'm starving," she groaned between mouthfuls. "I haven't eaten since breakfast."

Noah glanced at his watch, noting it was close to nine o'clock. "Don't wear yourself out. It's just a job." He sipped his drink.

"I can't help it. I feel so bad for them." She sucked on fingers covered in marinade. He shuffled uncomfortably in his seat.

She glanced around and then leaned closer to him. "I know they're doing it tough, but I honestly don't know how they're paying any of their bills."

The worry and fear she held for her employer touched him deeply. "Is it really that bad?"

"I shouldn't really be telling you this, but I'm worried about Dylan. I think he might be depressed. I've seen it before. Drought like this can cause even the strongest farmers to break down."

Noah mulled over what she was saying. When a farm or station was all you had, it was hard to go through such turbulent times. He had heard terrible statistics about rural suicide in Australia, but he didn't know Dylan, had never met him, so Noah couldn't speculate on his current state of mind.

He trusted Riley's judgement though. "Maybe I should tell Mum." He scratched his stubbled cheek. "She knows them well; she might be able to help him."

Riley exhaled in relief. "Thank you. I'd hate to hear that something bad happened." She laid her hand on his knee, and warmth spread though his body.

They joined in the group's conversation, sharing stories about Darcy. Noah laughed at the funny tales Darcy's friends shared. There were plenty of stories from his time on the campdrafting circuit.

Over the years, the brothers had exchanged regular letters and emails, and Darcy had kept Noah updated on the competitions he'd won. Noah had seen for himself the natural skill and talent Darcy possessed for the rodeo sport. But he had never prioritised it above Brigadier Station.

Now, hearing it from his friends, he understood how much Darcy had given up in order to help Lachie run the family property. But as he studied Darcy's happy expression, he could see his middle brother was happy with his choices.

With a few beers under his belt, Lachie started telling stories of his own. At first, they were funny tales of Darcy and their time together, but they soon turned to completely unrelated incidents where Lachie was the star.

"I was at the Birdsville Races years ago with a bunch of mates," Lachie slurred. "We decided to try our luck in the best-dressed competition."

Noah studied the crowd who had gathered to hear Lachie spin a yarn. They were star-struck by this larger-than-life figure. Where Noah and Darcy were introverted and quiet, Lachie was loud and rambunctious. He loved being the centre of attention, soaking it up, and he gained momentum the more followers he had. It was hard to live in the shadows of such a man.

A pretty young blonde in a short denim skirt sidled up against Lachie. He gave her a quick smile and put an arm around her as he continued regaling the group about the silly costumes he and his friends had worn at the desert horse race.

Unable to take any more, Noah shook his head and angled himself away.

Riley turned her head to him. "How about we go outside and get some fresh air? It's a bit noisy in here for me."

Noah smiled at her gratefully before collecting their drinks and going to the courtyard out back. They found two seats in a quiet corner, illuminated by glimmering fairy lights.

"Lachie sure does live up to his reputation," Riley said. "Has he always been like that?"

Noah picked up a cardboard coaster from the table and started toying with it, gently shredding the top layer. "He was like that as a teenager. Always the centre of attention. Always everyone's favourite."

Riley slid him a hooded gaze. "Is he the reason you moved away?"

Noah raised his head towards the door. He didn't have to tell her; he could leave and never speak of it.

Then he looked at her. Her long brown braid fell over her shoulder. He could see where it curled at the end.

"He was part of the reason. But mostly, it was our dad."

It was good to finally say it. He had held it in for such a long time, never letting anyone know the true reason he had left.

When Riley leaned over and placed her hand on his forearm, he expected to see pity, but instead he saw empathy and concern.

"Our dad was an alcoholic. He drank too much, yelled too much. Lachie never did anything wrong; he was the perfect child in Dad's eyes." Now he'd started, it was hard to stop. Years of pent-up emotion fell from his lips. "I broke my arm when I was six, and we told everyone it was because I fell off a horse. But it was Dad. He didn't even want to take me to the hospital. Said I deserved it. I can't remember what I did wrong now."

He stared at the shredded pieces of cardboard in front of him. The sound of his father's thunderous voice as clear and vivid as though it had happened yesterday.

He turned to Riley. Her brows were furrowed in concern, her eyes dark. Should he continue? What would she think of him when she knew everything?

She nodded slowly as if having read his mind and asking him to continue.

So he did. "He would blame us for everything, even the bloody weather. I let him take it out on me because then at least he would leave Mum alone. Then I got so angry. None of my friends got hit by their dads. So, I tried to fight back. But that just made it worse because that was what he wanted. He wanted me to fight back; he wanted me to hurt him the way he hurt me. I could see that in his eyes. Then I went to boarding school, and when I came home for the holidays, I could see Mum was hurt. She wore long sleeves in the middle of summer, and she limped around. Lachie didn't see it—of course he was always blind when it came to other people. But Darcy and I saw it, and we tried to get her to leave but she wouldn't. I don't know why; she could have stayed with friends or gone to the city. I doubt he would have followed her. I started to hate her for not helping herself. For not being strong enough. I started to imagine killing him. That's when I knew I had to leave."

Riley had put her free hand over her mouth. The hand on his forearm tightened.

"I realised that was not the person I wanted to be. So, when the opportunity to move to New Zealand with Jade came up, there was no question in my mind. I didn't want my life anymore. I wanted to go someplace where no one knew me, and no one knew him. And it worked." Noah looked down at his fingers and the tiny remains of the coaster.

Riley moved her hand up and down his arm. "I'm sorry you had to go through that. It's a terrible thing for a parent to do."

Noah bit his lip. He had opened his heart up like never before.

"What happened to your father?" Riley asked.

"Darcy wrote to me and said he had been found in one of the far paddocks. He'd had a heart attack." Noah paused as he remembered Darcy's letter. It had been hours later when Daniel's body had been found. He would have been alone and suffering for a while unable to call for help, the doctor had said. The one time Daniel hadn't taken the radio or the phone out with him had been the one time he'd really needed them.

"And you didn't come back for the funeral?"

Noah looked up to gaze at her face. She was so close, so beautiful. "I swore never to come back."

"But you're here now," she whispered, her eyes studying his like she could see into the deepest depths of his soul.

The gentle pressure of her hands on his arm did nothing to ease the world spinning around him. Knowing she was touching him only heightened the dizziness stealing his stability.

Her lips parted, and her breathing quickened. He shoved aside all thoughts of his father until nothing filled his mind but Riley Sinclair. Her smell, her voice, the alluring way she looked at him.

"Thank you for telling me," she whispered.

"Thank you for listening." His blood pounded through his veins. He had never wanted anyone the way he wanted her. The way he needed her. All she had to do was smile and the self-control he prided himself on would snap.

The door to the pub burst open and filled the courtyard with music and laughter. Riley turned with a start, the magic of the moment broken between them.

CHAPTER 8

*A*t first light, Riley had driven to the aero club, itching to get back into the sky. She lovingly ran her hands over her shiny bird before fuelling up and going through her pre-flight checklist, and then starting the motor. Lifting from the ground, she watched the dirt swirl beneath her.

The small township of Julia Creek made way for barren stretches of land. She couldn't help but be mesmerised by the undulating scenery beneath her. Cattle meandered below as she ventured farther out of town and then were replaced by the fluffy white specks of sheep as she flew over Dylan's property.

Swinging to the east, she decided to circle over Brigadier Station, her mind still churning with what Noah had told her last night. A childhood like that could leave a person emotionally damaged. It broke her heart to think of the horror he must have gone through. In a way, it made her appreciate her own childhood more. Her mother and father hadn't been around, but at least she hadn't had to suffer at their hands.

The ground below her was baked hard and cracked in places; all the dams were critically low or dry. Something needed to be done. It needed to rain.

Then she spotted a man watching her from a shady spot under a huge gum tree. He stepped out into the sun, removed his hat, and waved at her.

Riley smiled and, finding a clear patch, landed on the dirt floor. She powered the helicopter down and climbed out, meeting Noah as he walked towards her.

"Morning." He nodded at the chopper. "You spying on us?"

She grinned and took in his dirty jeans and blue shirt. He must have been working for hours already to be so dirty. "She needed a spin. Can't leave a heli idle for too long."

He gestured at the Land Cruiser behind him. "I have coffee in a thermos. Do you want some?"

She nodded, and together they headed to the vehicle. Their arms brushed as they walked, sending little jolts of fire up her arms.

Noah poured her a cup of steaming black coffee, and she swallowed the bitter liquid, feeling her stomach warm.

"Early morning start?" she asked. She followed his gaze to the fence line where tools were scattered around a gaping hole.

"Just doing some jobs that have been overlooked. Save Lachie having to do it later."

"How did he fare after last night?"

Lachie had been quite far gone when Noah had loaded him into the Land Cruiser. "Pretty ordinary."

Noah drank deeply from the thermos and Riley watched his long, stubble-covered throat move as he swallowed. "So, what are your plans after the wedding?" he asked.

Riley bit her lip, she'd been paying way too much attention to his mouth and throat. "I don't plan too far ahead. Grant will let me know when the next job comes in. I'll probably head back to Longreach until then."

"Is Longreach home?" His gaze narrowed on her.

"Well, Grant lives there with his girlfriend. I keep my stuff in their spare room. So, I guess that's home." It had been a long time since she had lived anywhere long enough to call it home. To put down roots.

Riley finished off her cup and nodded towards the helicopter. "Fancy a ride?" She blushed as his eyes darkened. "In my helicopter. Do you want to come for a fly?"

He let out a deep chuckle. Oh, she could get lost in the sound of his laughter.

"I dunno." He smiled and winked at her. "Your fancy flying might be too much for my sensitive masculine ego."

His teasing was infectious. She pouted and fluttered her eyelashes girlishly at him. "Is the big, strong cowboy scared?"

He put the thermos down. "Maybe I am."

She slowly started walking backwards. "Are you afraid of heights?"

Slowly, he followed her. "Not of heights."

"The helicopter?" She lengthened her strides.

He shook his head.

She stopped, and he moved forward until they were within touching distance. "Are you scared of falling?"

"I am." His hands ran gently up her arms, sending sensations to the tips of her fingers. Swallowing, she looked into his face. His eyes were on her lips. Blood pounded past her ears, loud and intense. Everything tightened, from the tiniest muscle in her body to the very air surrounding them. As if the world held its breath, hopeful.

She couldn't remember ever wanting to kiss someone so badly. Her body swayed, weight shifting to the balls of her feet. She placed a moist hand on his chest, feeling his heart thump beneath it. Her pumping blood became a roar.

"I'm scared of falling for you," he said, his voice husky and deep.

Then his mouth was on hers, devouring her. His hands tangled in her hair. Fire ignited every sense while at the same time her skin shivered with goose bumps.

When they finally pulled apart, she took a moment to catch her breath. "What was that for?"

He smiled back at her and stroked her cheek. The crystal clearness of his blue eyes held her transfixed. "I had to know what that would be like," he said with a hint of a smile. "You know, in case we die."

She laughed and gently pushed him back. "Come on then. I'll show you just what I can do."

Riley opened the passenger door and motioned for Noah

to climb in. He did as she beckoned and couldn't help but suppress a smile as she all but climbed over him to click in his H seat belt. She patted it against his chest and grinned broadly at him. "Safe and secure now," she said.

Her smile made him want to kiss her again. Hard and long and breathlessly.

He had spent last night worried he had missed his chance to find out what was between them. He had sworn to himself that if he got the opportunity again, he would kiss her.

She hadn't rejected him. She had kissed him back, and it had blown his mind.

She closed his door, and he took the opportunity to study all the knobs and controllers in front of him. He was surprised so much could fit in such a small space.

Climbing in next to him, she put on her own seat belt, and started pressing buttons. She reached out and pulled down two headsets and handed one of them to him. He put it on and moved the mouthpiece in front of his lips as the sound of the helicopter starting up eliminated all the other noises.

Noah watched as Riley became all serious and professional, so different from just a few minutes ago when she had been cheeky and playful, flirtatious, and sexy as all hell. But this skilled side of her was a turn-on too.

Riley did something to him, aroused feelings he couldn't stop, made him act in ways he couldn't help. He wanted her, no question.

He watched out the window as they gently lifted off the ground, the Land Cruiser becoming smaller the higher they went. Adrenalin pumped through him and his stomach tightened. And as stunning as the scenery beneath him was, he couldn't help but be entranced by the woman beside him. Her feet danced on the foot controls as her hand moved the cyclic in front of her. She seemed to do it all by feel, not once taking her eyes from the window.

"You make it look easy."

She glanced over at him and smiled. "Trust me, if it was easy, everyone would do it."

He relaxed into his seat as she flew gentle circles around Brigadier Station. But before he could get too content with the easy sightseeing tour, she accelerated. Noah's stomach lurched. *Holy shit!*

After bringing the machine quite low to the ground, she then pulled back on the cyclic, making the machine lift quickly. Just as he was recovering from that, she did some sharp turns which made him bite his tongue to stop himself calling out.

Noah was relieved he had skipped breakfast that morning, and as Riley finally brought the helicopter down, his stomach started to settle.

She didn't turn the engine off. Instead, she turned to him and spoke into the mic. "You okay?"

He nodded, unsure of his voice.

She unbuckled her seat belt and leaned over to him. She moved the microphones away from their mouths before kissing him softly. His stomach flip-flopped, but this time, in a good way. He placed his hands on her arms, wanting to deepen the kiss. To take as much as she offered. His desire swelled, and he shifted in his seat, his jeans uncomfortably tight.

She moaned against his mouth. "I've gotta get back to work."

He dragged himself away from her. She was right. As much as he would like to do dirty things to her right there in the cockpit, there was work to be done and he needed to get on with it.

He unbuckled his seat belt and removed his headset. "See you at the wedding and thanks for the ride," he shouted over the humming engine.

"See? You're still in one piece," she replied with a grin.

Yep, one very hot, turned-on piece. He climbed down and firmly closed the door behind him.

He looked back in at her, sitting in the cockpit, so professional and sexy. She smiled and blew him a kiss.

He backed up to a safe distance, and then watched as she expertly lifted the machine into the sky. She circled widely and dipped as though waving at him. Then she was flying away and into the horizon, and he was left staring at the cloudless blue sky over Brigadier Station.

CHAPTER 9

*R*iley collapsed, exhausted, onto the bed. She yawned and stretched her arms, feeling her muscles tighten and relax. When she was flying, it was a different kind of exhaustion to this bone-wearisome tiredness from hard, physical labour. Flying was a mental game, the mind always hard at work, knowing that making the wrong decision could mean hours of extra work, or worse yet, result in a serious accident.

She felt a tremendous sense of accomplishment from the day's work. She hoped she had done enough to help the struggling family. A week just hadn't been long enough.

Excitement and anticipation flickered through her as she turned her thoughts to the following day's activities. She would accompany Dylan's family to Arabella Plains early tomorrow morning so they could attend Darcy and Meghan's wedding. Normally, she didn't care for fancy formal events. But the wedding of her good friend was an exception. Plus, Noah would be there.

She closed her eyes and relived the kisses they had shared that morning. She moaned as she remembered the expert way his mouth had moved over hers and thought of all the other places on her body where she wouldn't mind feeling those lips. Blood rushed through her veins, igniting all her senses.

The piercing ringtone of her mobile cut into her fantasy. She groaned as she retrieved it from her back pocket.

"Hey, Grant. What's up?"

"Just giving you the heads up that the job in Charleville got canned." Her cousin was, as usual, all professional and businesslike.

"Bummer. How come?" Riley sat up. It had been a promising government contract that they had tendered for. The six-month project would have kept both helicopters busy and brought in a substantial wage.

"Who knows? It's all politics and government red tape," he said on a sigh. "So, no need to hurry back."

There was nothing waiting for her in Longreach, and she wouldn't mind staying around Julia Creek and spending some more time with Noah. "I'll find something to do. How's Andrea?"

"Good, we're all good. Nothing much changes here." Grant's voice softened as he spoke of his girlfriend. "What about up there? How's the wedding visit going?"

"Great actually. The wedding's tomorrow." She absently traced the patterns on the doona with her fingertip.

There was a brief pause on the end of the line. "What's up, Ry?"

She could never hide anything from Grant, especially when it came to her love life. He and Andrea were constantly trying to set her up and convince her just how great being part of a couple was. She appreciated that they did it out of love for her, but sometimes, she just wished they'd stay out of her business.

"It's nothing. Don't worry about it."

"Who is he?" Grant probed, his voice full of amusement.

She sighed, knowing he wouldn't give up until he had all the details to pass onto Andrea. "Well, it turns out Darcy has a younger brother."

"And?"

"And he's a lot like Darcy, only younger and hotter," she explained, thinking about how well Noah filled out his denim jeans.

"So, what's the problem then? You've got time to kill now. You might as well have some fun," Grant encouraged. "Unless he's married."

"No, he's not married." She squirmed on the bed. "I don't think he'd be into a casual relationship."

"Does it have to be casual? Maybe he could be the one."

"Come on, Grant. You know me better than anyone. I'm not looking for someone to hold me down."

"He doesn't have to hold you down, Ry. Andrea doesn't stop me from doing what I love."

"I'm sorry. I know she doesn't." Riley loved Andrea like a sister and admired the woman greatly. She never complained about Grant's long hours and risky career. "But it's different with guys. How would you feel if you were a cattleman and the girl you were dating was a helicopter pilot who travelled as much as me?"

"Yeah, I get what you're saying, but give him a chance. He might be different."

Riley chewed on the inside of her cheek.

"What are you really afraid of?" her cousin asked.

"It's just that, I don't know. If I was going to settle down with someone," she admitted, "it would be with someone like him."

"Wow. You've never said anything like that before."

"I know. It scares me because I don't want to settle down. Ever."

"A lifetime is a long time to spend without someone to love." Grant's voice had been filled with love as he uttered the most profound words she had ever heard him speak.

Riley couldn't help but laugh. "Did you read that on a fortune cookie?"

"Maybe." He laughed back. "Talk to him. He might surprise you."

"Yeah, okay. Like you said, maybe we can just have a little bit of fun for a while."

Riley knew they could have a lot of fun together; the chemistry between them promised it would be amazing. But she had the niggling sensation that someone would get hurt when it inevitably ended. And, as much as she was worried that that person would be her, she was even more worried that it would be Noah. The idea that she might cause him pain was something that truly scared her.

reshly showered and still buzzing from his morning with Riley, Noah felt like whistling as he joined his family for dinner. The kitchen was abuzz with anticipation as Lachie carved the meat and Harriet tossed a salad together.

"What can I do to help?" he asked, gently placing a hand on his mother's shoulder.

She smiled affectionately at him. "There's garlic bread in the oven. Can you take it out and put it on the table?"

He did as she asked, unwrapping the loaves from the tin foil and placing them on a plate before carrying it into the adjoining dining room.

The table was set for four tonight. Harriet had asked that it just be her and her three sons on the eve of the long-anticipated wedding. Freshly cut flowers filled a vase in the centre of the table, filling the room with their sweet, feminine scent.

Darcy stepped in from the verandah, a can of soft drink in his hand. "G'day, Noah."

The brothers greeted each other with a handshake.

"So how does it feel? Are you nervous about tomorrow?" Noah asked.

Darcy grinned and shook his head. "What is there to be nervous about? I finally get to marry the girl of my dreams."

Noah slapped his brother on the back. "I really am happy for you two. Congratulations." He couldn't help but be a little envious of just how happy Darcy looked. Like he really was the luckiest man in the world.

Darcy raised an eyebrow. "How are you and Riley going?"

"What 'me and Riley'? There is no me and Riley."

Darcy's grin was wide, and his eyes were dancing. "I saw the way you two watched each other; I'm not blind. To be honest, I've never seen her look at anyone the way she looks at you."

Noah let his brother's observations sink in. Had it really been that obvious? Until this morning, he hadn't been sure of anything.

He was already yearning to see her again. To taste more of her, to find out all her dreams and desires.

The brothers took their seats as Harriet and Lachie placed plates of food on the table. It all looked and smelled so good.

"You've outdone yourself tonight, Mum," Darcy said with a smile.

"It's not often I get to cook for all three of my sons." She gazed over the table. "Noah, can I get you a drink? There are plenty of soft drinks in the fridge."

"I'll get it." He stood and motioned for her to sit down.

"Grab me a beer while you're up, would you?" Lachie asked.

"No alcohol," Harriet said, using that voice from their childhood—that   don't-even-think-about-arguing-with-me tone.

"Come on, Mum," Lachie complained. "Just one."

"Absolutely not. It's the night before your brother's wedding, and no one is drinking any alcohol." Harriet's tone was fierce and unrelenting.

The men glanced questioningly at each other.

"How are we supposed to toast Darcy, then?" Lachie asked.

"We can toast him with a soft drink." Harriet's tone sweetened.

Noah slipped away to the fridge and pulled out two cans of Coke. What was his mother up to and what was she planning for the night? Maybe it was an intervention for Lachie? God knew he needed one.

"What's Meghan doing tonight, Darcy?" Harriet asked as they ate their meals.

"Her friend Jodie drove out this afternoon so the two of them are having a girl's night in," Darcy explained.

"Knowing Jodie, they'll be busy with facials and pedicures all night," Lachie said.

"I heard Meghan say something about *Magic Mike*, but I have no idea what she meant." Darcy shrugged as he finished off his meal.

"Who's Jodie?" Noah asked.

"Meghan's best friend from Townsville," Harriet said.

"Here's to a successful second attempt." Lachie raised his can in a salute before taking a swig.

Noah frowned at Darcy.

"Jodie was also supposed to be maid of honour at their wedding." Darcy gestured at Lachie.

Noah nodded, understanding. Lachie was dealing with the situation well, all things considered. It must feel a bit like déjà vu, except this time he wasn't the groom.

As the meal came to a close, Harriet clinked her spoon against her glass of water. Her sons looked at her expectantly.

"I'm so happy to have all three of you under the same roof tonight. It's been a long time. Too long." She paused and looked at each of her sons in turn. "Darcy, I know you and Meghan are going to be very happy together. Lachie, it is admirable the way you have handled this situation. It shows great maturity and love for your brother." Harriet turned to Noah, and her eyes misted over. "Noah, I'm sorry that you felt you had to leave here all those years ago and that we missed out on that time with you. I understand why you did leave, and I'm sorry."

Noah squirmed uncomfortably in his seat, dropping his gaze to the table.

"You boys have all waited a long time for me to tell you the truth about your father, and I think you all deserve to hear the real story.

"I was seventeen when I married your father. I was young, and I thought I was in love. Daniel was very handsome and came from a good family. But he wasn't in love with me; it was my best friend, Enid, who he wanted. She'd turned him down, so he redirected his attention to me and proposed on our second date."

Noah vaguely remembered hearing a similar story as a

child. Daniel proposing on the second date had seemed like the ultimate love story back then. Before he knew what his father was really like.

"I knew he enjoyed his drink, and it just got worse after the wedding. He would have a beer or two in the evening to help him relax, but it didn't take long for one or two drinks to become a twelve-pack or even more."

Noah glanced at his brothers, expecting them to be shocked, but it was recognition and resignation that showed on Lachie's face. It was as if his expression said the spiral their father had followed was as familiar as his own.

"He then started having a scotch in the mornings —'hair of the dog' he would call it. Once he started doing that …" She shrugged, needing no further explanation. "Whenever I questioned him about it, he would yell at me. So I stopped mentioning it altogether."

Noah knew this about his father, but it was a relief to hear her say it out loud. Lachie was sitting quite still and had paled significantly.

"Daniel was verbally abusive in the early years, but it wasn't until after Darcy was born that he started getting physical." A single tear slipped silently down Harriet's ivory cheek.

"It's okay, Mum. You can stop," Darcy said, patting her hand.

"No, you need to hear this." She sniffed before turning to her youngest son. "Noah, your father always treated you differently because he felt guilty. The night you were conceived …" She paused to take a deep breath. "That night, we had a huge fight and he beat me. Then he … he raped me."

Noah recoiled in horror.

"Mum, I'm so sorry," Darcy's voice quivered.

Lachie stood and started pacing around the room. Both the brothers' faces were twisted in a combination of anguish and disgust.

Noah raked his hands through his hair, his whole body shaking with the force of his feelings.

"It was never your fault, Noah," Harriet continued. "It was Daniel's. You were a reminder of what he had done. The guilt ate away at him, so he numbed himself from it by drinking more. There was nothing you ever could have done that would have made him treat you any differently. You need to know that."

Noah felt frozen to his chair, unable to move even if he'd wanted to. Deep down, he had always known there was a reason why he was different. Sometimes he had wondered if Daniel was actually his father. But he knew his mother well enough to know she would never have been unfaithful.

He had been conceived in hate and fear. Now he knew the truth, everything was clear. It all made sense. That's why his father had detested him.

"If only he had gotten help in those early days, we could have been so happy." Harriet took Noah's hand in hers and squeezed. "But he's gone now, and I want you boys to learn from his mistakes. None of you need to be like him."

"Why did you put up with that, Mum?" Lachie stopped pacing. "How did I never know he was so evil?"

They all looked expectantly at Harriet.

"He hid that side of himself from you, Lachie. He hid it from most people. Because of that, I knew no one would ever believe me if I told them what he did to me. To us. Daniel was an upstanding member of the community. He was on committees and councils. Respected and adored. He wasn't the kind of man who would beat and abuse his wife and children." Harriet's voice broke. "I couldn't leave without you boys, and he told me often enough that he would kill me if I tried. So, I did what I had to do. As long as he targeted me, you three would be okay. But I couldn't stop him from hurting Noah." She turned to him then. "I was relieved when you left. Happy you got away to safety, even though it meant I couldn't see you." She paused, a steady stream of tears flowing down her cheeks. "You boys are the best thing that ever happened to me. I would do anything for you. I love you all so much."

Darcy hugged her first. Noah stood and went second. She pulled him close and hugged them both at once. He closed his eyes as he let his own emotion wash through him. Harriet had suffered at his father's hand too. She'd put up with it much longer than him, and in a time before there was much support for women in abusive relationships. She had been through so much but still managed to put on a smile and shower her family with love. He would never blame her for the past again.

After several long minutes, they broke apart. Noah's body was heavy with exhaustion.

"I'm going to turn in," Harriet said. "I'll do the dishes in the morning."

"We'll do them, Mum," Lachie said and hugged her briefly.

She nodded before moving off down the hallway to her bedroom.

"I wasn't expecting that." Darcy sighed as he collapsed into his chair.

Lachie leaned on the doorframe with his arms crossed. "Did you know, Darcy?"

"Not the whole story, but I knew he hit her." Darcy glanced at Noah. "He hurt us too. Remember all the bruises I mysteriously got during the school holidays?"

"Shit, I'm sorry." Lachie thrust his hand through his hair. "How bad was it for you, Noah?"

Noah studied the floor as he spoke. Harriet was right; they deserved to know the truth. "I never did anything right. He found the smallest excuses to punch and hit me. I watched him hurt Mum too. I had to leave. I couldn't protect myself, and I couldn't protect her. I knew that if I didn't leave, I would have killed the son of a bitch."

Silence fell and Noah contemplated the truth and how it might affect their lives going forward.

"It's a good thing he's dead." Lachie's voice was firm and unwavering as he stared into the centre of the table. "If I had known what he'd done, I would have killed him myself."

$\mathcal{N}$oah had a restless night's sleep, still reeling from Harriet's revelations about his birth. In some ways, it was a relief to know the truth—that he had never personally done anything to make his father hate him. Daniel hadn't been able to fight his demons—he'd made too many bad mistakes, hurt too many people. People he was supposed to protect and love.

As Noah dressed in his formal black trousers and jacket, he resolved to take a break from thinking about it. At least for today. Today was all about Darcy and Meghan. About welcoming his new sister into the family.

Thoughts of Riley brightened his sombre mood. What was she doing right now? Would she be wearing a dress to the wedding like the other women or, stubborn as she was, would she attend in her usual jeans and shirt? He'd like to see her in a dress. Something short, he hoped, so he could see her legs.

He remembered the way she'd made his pulse race and his hands sweaty and had him tripping over his words and responding in unusual ways. Normally he wouldn't trust someone so quickly, especially with his heart. But there was something about Riley that made him comfortable. Like she would keep his secrets and help him through his dark times. He had never met anyone like her before.

In the kitchen, he helped himself to a cup of tea and cereal before sitting down next to Lachie who was munching on some toast.

Their mother was busy packing bags and doing last-minute preparations so they could leave. Her demeanour was bright and cheerful despite last night's revelations.

"Someone's excited then." Lachie laughed at his mother as she bustled out of the room.

"She probably doubted any of us would ever get married." Noah smiled.

Lachie chuckled. "Especially after my fiasco. Lucky you weren't here for that."

Noah turned to his brother, a wave of sympathy overcoming him. "That must've been tough, mate, what happened. Good on you for handling it the way you did."

"I didn't handle it that well. I crashed the quad. But, in hindsight, it happened the way it was supposed to happen. Meghan's much better off with Darcy." Maturity seemed to have hardened Lachie's features overnight. "What went wrong with you and Jade?"

Noah scratched nervously behind his ear. "I think we just grew apart. In the end, we both wanted different things. She's got a new guy now and is really happy. To be honest, I really don't have much to go back to in New Zealand."

"Well, it's been a real help you being here. You will always be welcome at Brigadier Station. I might even pay you if you do a good enough job." Lachie smiled. A teasing glint twinkled in his eye.

"Maybe when Darcy and Meghan get back." Noah shrugged.

Lachie stared into his bowl and spoke quietly. "I've been thinking, after what Mum said last night—I should give up the drink. I don't want to be like Dad."

Noah studied his brother. Lachie had never looked so vulnerable and honest before. "That's very brave. We will all help and support you however we can."

Lachie looked up and nodded slowly. "Thanks."

"Mum, take a breath," Darcy said in the direction of the kitchen, then walked into the room.

Noah took the opportunity to really look at his two brothers. Both in their thirties now, they were tall and slim, dressed in black jackets and trousers with white shirts and blue ties. Despite their father, the Brigadier boys had turned out okay. If they'd made it through the trials they had already faced, they could surely make it through anything else that life might throw their way. Noah smiled. This was his family.

This was home.

Noah pulled at his collar. The late afternoon sun still had a bite to it.

The couple had wanted a small, intimate wedding, and

as Noah waited alongside his family, he hoped it would play out as planned.

The courtyard garden at Arabella Plains was in full spring bloom. The tropical plants mingled with the colourful rosebushes. The grass below them was lush and green, and the gum trees overhead sheltered the gathered congregation. Squawking parrots and kookaburras performed a background symphony which could just be heard above the chatter of the excited guests.

As the celebrant and Darcy took their positions, Noah, Lachie, and his mother stood to await the bride. Noah caught a glimpse of blue and turned just in time to see Riley hurry up the aisle and take her seat. He found himself gawking at the short, figure-hugging, turquoise dress she wore. He felt a bit sheepish when she caught him staring, but he couldn't help himself. Her hair was loose and brushed her bare shoulders, and his fingers itched to touch her, to feel her smooth skin against his own.

A familiar country tune started to play, and everyone looked towards the house. The door opened, and Meghan stepped out onto the verandah.

Her gown was elegant and simple, with capped sleeves and a tapered waist. Delicate embroided flowers adorned the sheer, floor-length fabric. In front of her, she clutched a bouquet of colourful roses and as she stepped into the light, her dress shimmered and sparkled. Not a trace of anxiety appeared on her face—only happiness as she focused on the man waiting for her at the front of the alter.

When she reached Darcy, he took her hand and they

looked longingly into each other's eyes. Noah's vision blurred as the emotions from the last few weeks overcame him.

The celebrant performed the brief ceremony and the vows and rings were exchanged and Noah couldn't help but envy the obvious love and affection for each other that the couple radiated.

He found himself turning to seek Riley out from across the aisle. She looked caught up in the romance and magic of the moment. It gave him hope that perhaps this was something she might one day want as well. And when her eyes met his, he couldn't bring himself to look away— he was so hypnotised by the moment and the strength of their attraction to each other.

He didn't know how long they sat gazing at each other, but suddenly he was aware that the crowd was cheering, and everyone was standing as the newly pronounced bride and groom walked down the aisle hand-in-hand.

Waiting for the chance to be with Riley was killing him. She was so close but so far away with everyone around them. His hands ached to touch her. He wanted to draw her close and let her know how much he wanted her.

Noah followed his mother and when it was his turn to congratulate the newlyweds, he shook his brother's hand and hugged his new sister.

"Congratulations," Noah said. "You two will be so happy together."

"Thank you." Meghan smiled brightly. "And thank you for looking after the station while we're away. I'm sorry if it's inconvenient."

"Not at all, I'm happy to do it. I owe it to Darcy," he said, thinking of all his brother had done for him growing up.

"Well, I hope you'll treat it like your home. You're welcome here whenever you like. We are family after all." Meghan's words warmed his heart. They were truly blessed to have gained such a wonderful new family member.

He stepped aside so the next eager guest could bestow their well-wishes. He turned to gaze upon the crowd, easily spotting Riley, and taking the opportunity to fully appreciate the close-fitting dress. He hadn't realised just how long and slender her legs were. Her shoulders were uncovered for a change and showed off the well-toned muscles in her arms. Noah grabbed a champagne flute from a tray a waitress was holding. Despite not having a taste for the fizzy stuff, he downed it quickly.

For Dutch courage.

As Noah took a gulp of champagne, Riley couldn't help her gaze following his muscled arms and locking on his mouth. An almost painful ache squeezed her chest. This was the man who had haunted her thoughts ever since she'd met him. Had it really only been one week? Here they were, back at Arabella Plains where it had all begun such a short time ago, but it already felt like she knew him better than she knew anyone else—even Darcy.

The line inched forward slowly. Well-wishers took

their time to share this special moment and bestow their congratulations on the beautiful, happy couple.

Riley never cried at weddings. Well, she hadn't cried at the only other two she had ever attended. But this wedding and this couple had truly tested her feminine sensitivity. Darcy and Meghan were just so perfectly suited, with common interests and ideals. Their relationship was built on trust, honesty and respect. Her greatest hope for them was that they never lost sight of those foundations.

When her turn finally came, she gave Darcy a wide grin and a tight squeeze. "Congratulations."

"Thanks, Riley." Then, holding her at arm's length, he made a point of studying her in the turquoise dress. "Wow."

She groaned before bursting into laughter and poking him in the ribs. "Apparently jeans and a T-shirt aren't formal enough for this event."

"Even if you ironed that western shirt, it still wouldn't have been formal enough for a wedding," Meghan chimed in from beside her husband before pulling Riley into a warm embrace. "You look stunning."

"Thanks. I'll return it to Jodie before I leave." Riley stood back and gestured at Meghan and her sparkly white dress. "You look amazing, and what a beautiful ceremony."

"Thank you." Meghan clutched her husband's hand and they gazed lovingly into each other's eyes.

"We couldn't have asked for a better day." Darcy lowered his head and kissed his bride.

"Get a room, you two." Noah groaned from behind

Riley's shoulder, and she turned to see his cheeky expression.

The two lovebirds were caught up in their special moment so Riley joined Noah, who promptly handed her a glass of champagne. She took a sip, enjoying the bubbles fizzing on her tongue, and licked her lips, tasting the lipstick Jodie had painted on her that afternoon.

"That's a hell of a dress," Noah said softly. He was tantalisingly close; she could feel his breath on her neck.

She watched through her lashes as his eyes roamed over her. "It's one of Jodie's. Not really my style."

"You look great in it." His voice was husky and deep. "But you would look great in anything."

She shivered at his words, so full of longing. She swallowed the rest of the champagne. There was so much she wanted to do to him. So much she wanted him to do to her. But this was not the time or the place for those urges to become reality.

"When do you go back to Brigadier Station?" she asked.

Noah took a small step backwards and cleared his throat. "I'm house-sitting this place for the next month." He gestured to the weatherboard homestead.

"Lucky you. It looks like a great place to stay." She raised her eyebrow suggestively.

"Yep. It's got all the mod cons. Hot water. Dishwasher. Might be a bit lonely though, just me and the horses."

Was he propositioning her? She studied his eyes and saw a hint of vulnerability in them.

"Will you come and visit me? Maybe you could join me for dinner one night?"

She nodded before she could stop herself. "I'd like that." She closed the gap between them, and their mouths touched slowly and gently. It was a quick kiss. A taste of what could come.

"Riley!" A tall blonde woman stopped next to them with her hands on her hips. "Who is this?"

"Jodie, haven't you met Darcy's other brother?" Riley smiled at Meghan's unofficial maid of honour. The couple had decided not to have attendants as it would have been too hard to choose between Noah and Lachie, or that was what Jodie had told her.

Noah shook Jodie's slender hand and introduced himself.

"I can't believe the genes of this family. Thank you, Mrs McGuire." Jodie winked at Riley, who laughed at her brazenness.

"You two have fun. I'll catch you later," Jodie said before turning on her high heels and striding off, no doubt in search of a more available man.

Noah smothered a chuckle with his hand.

"She's from the city," Riley said as though that would explain everything. "She means well."

The ceremony was followed by a casual cocktail-style dinner. The guests mingled, and everyone appeared happy and jovial.

Riley stayed close to Noah, enjoying the familiar warmth of his presence. He didn't complain and took the opportunity to casually take her hand and hold it between his own calloused workman's ones. It felt surprisingly pleasant and natural to Riley who couldn't remember the last time she had held someone's hand.

Lachie ambled over, steadily sipping on a bottle of Coke. He glanced at their intertwined hands before sending a quizzical look at Noah.

"We haven't been properly introduced. I'm Lachie," he said.

"Riley Sinclair." She smiled at him. He was pretty drunk the night they had met at the pub and they hadn't spoken so she wasn't surprised he didn't remember her.

"Riley is a good friend of Darcy's," Noah said.

"Nice to meet you." Lachie smiled a long, lazy smile that had probably swept many women off their feet and into his arms. But it wouldn't work on Riley. There was only one McGuire brother she wanted.

She rubbed her hand up Noah's arm and he relaxed under her reassuring touch. He had nothing to worry about.

"Did you see Mum? I've never seen her so happy." Lachie said.

"She sure is." Noah had an almost dreamlike quality to his voice. He was, Riley had to admit, looking stupidly sexy in his black trousers and white shirt that hugged his chest and showed off his broad shoulders. The black jacket he had worn for the ceremony had been removed as the heat of the afternoon beat down on them. Most of the men in attendance had done the same.

"So, Riley, Darcy told me you're a helicopter pilot. How long have you been doing that?" Lachie turned enquiring eyes to her.

"Straight out of school. My cousin, Grant, helped me fund my way; he was already a pilot, and we made plans to work together."

"That's a pretty fearless career you've chosen. Have you had any close calls?"

Riley bit her lip and debated whether to be completely honest in front of Noah. She could tell him about all the near misses and accidents she and Grant had been involved in or she could do what she normally did and brush it off. "I've had my share of close calls." She chose her words carefully. "It's not exactly the safest career choice, but I keep up with my training and always practice safety first."

Lachie nodded his head approvingly. "I admire you. Darcy reckons flying is pretty amazing, but I don't even like to be a passenger."

"Noah wasn't too keen to come up with me the other day either." She smiled when Noah's face redden slightly.

Lachie turned his teasing eyes on his little brother. "Jeez, you didn't spew, did you? How embarrassing."

Noah pushed his brother playfully. "Of course not. I reckon you would have though. She sure knows how to push a man to the limits."

"I bet she does," Lachie muttered the words to his brother.

The afternoon progressed into the early evening, and Noah and Riley found themselves ambling towards the yards where the horses were kept. They leaned on the wooden railings and watched the animals graze peacefully.

Riley contemplated the sunset, glorious against the undisturbed landscape. Across the paddocks came the occasional horse whinny. She could get used to this lifestyle, Riley realised, and the thought didn't scare her as much as it once might have.

Noah held out a hand and made a clicking noise at the horses. He was rewarded when one brown and white appaloosa looked his way before trotting towards them.

He spoke sweet nothings to the horse as he tickled its chin and whiskers.

"You can pat her. She won't bite." He smiled at Riley.

Riley leaned in close to Noah, resting her body against his shoulder, and scratched behind the horse's ear. "She's gorgeous."

"This is Zephyr. She's one of Darcy's newest horses."

"Hello, Zephyr." Riley inhaled deeply and let the familiar horse smell seep into her senses.

"Do you ride?" He turned his head towards her and his warm breath brushed her forehead. She looked up and gazed at his mouth—that full, lush mouth. She swallowed.

"When I get a chance to. I've always had a soft spot for horses," she admitted.

"We should go for a ride when you come visit me then."

She nodded and dropped her hand from the horse.

His touch was gentle as he drew her closer, moving his body towards her. His warm finger traced the angles of her face softly and her heart pounded in her ears. His rapid, shallow breaths caused her attention to slip to his mouth. Then he started to lower his head. She closed her eyes a second before their lips touched.

The kiss could only be described as mind-blowing. They stayed, holding and kissing one another as the sun sank below the horizon. The rhythm of their breathing and the sound of the appaloosa's legs brushing through the grass created a soundtrack for the moment.

"Noah?"

He turned his head to look at her and caught a glimpse of hope and want and a thousand other things he longed for but wasn't sure whether to believe.

He pressed a kiss to her forehead and smoothed her hair against her head. Nothing would ruin this perfect moment or this perfect day. He didn't want to think about his mother's revelations. His father's history. He didn't want to reveal his growing attraction to Riley in case it scared her away. His feelings were so fragile, his emotions so vulnerable. He just wanted to stay in this moment forever, holding this warm, beautiful woman in his arms.

"We should re-join the party." Her voice was soft.

"We should," he agreed reluctantly.

She let her arms drop from his back, but clasped his hand tightly as though knowing he required this reassurance and comfort.

They didn't need words. They just needed each other.

CHAPTER 12

*T*he soft neighing of the horses pulled Noah from his deep slumber as his mind hovered between sleep and consciousness. When had he last slept so well?

Memories of the night before slowly seeped to the surface. He smiled as he remembered being with Riley. Kissing her and tasting her luscious, full lips.

The wedding party had continued well after midnight. With hands held, they had chatted to their neighbours while a local country band had played. Meghan and Darcy had cut their cake and shared their first dance amidst the cheers and clapping of their closest friends and family.

When Riley had started yawning, they had slipped away together, setting his swag out on the hay in the stables. Warmth spread over him at the memory of falling asleep with Riley tucked snugly against his body. The smells of her hair and the hay had coaxed him to sleep.

He peeked through his lashes. She was still there. Nothing more than kisses had occurred last night, and his body still ached for her. He yearned to explore hers, to feel it all under his touch. Cautiously, he raised his twitching fingers and combed them gently through her silky hair.

She turned into his hand. The hint of a smile stretched over her face. "Noah."

His heart pounded at the sound of his name from her mouth. Had she been dreaming about him? Did she want him as much as he wanted her?

She reached out her hand, placed it on his hip, and shuffled her body closer. Heat radiated between them. Then she opened her eyes and gazed deeply into his. For several seconds, they looked at each other, lost in the depths, each searching for answers to the questions neither wanted to ask.

"Good morning." Her lips curved in a smile.

"Morning. Did you sleep well?" Unable to keep his hands from her, he stroked her arm.

"So well. I haven't slept in a man's arms in—" She paused and frowned slightly. "I don't know how long."

He dropped his voice suggestively. "Happy to be of service."

She giggled, and the sound warmed his heart. He brushed a light kiss on her lips and moved his hand along the curve of her arm. Desire quivered in his stomach. He dropped his head again. This time her lips clung to him, deepening the kiss, devouring him.

But this was not where he wanted to make love to her for the first time, so with a groan, he let her go.

Sighing, Riley rolled over and unzipped the swag. Noah took the opportunity to admire her well-defined back, hips, and perfectly pert bottom. The turquoise dress rode high up her thighs, and he glimpsed black underwear before she pulled it down.

"I need to find a bathroom and change."

"You'll have to go to the house." He sat and looked at his watch. "Mum will be cooking breakfast for everyone."

"Ugh, walk-of-shame time then."

Noah stood and rolled up the swag while Riley collected her bag from Dylan's unlocked car. They met again a few minutes later just outside the kitchen door.

The chatter and laughter was so intense it sounded like everyone from the wedding had come back for Harriet's famous pancakes. Noah took a deep breath before opening the door and letting Riley go in ahead of him.

As he'd expected, everyone turned to see who the newcomers were. Lachie wolf whistled, and cheers went up from the men.

"Now, now," Harriet's voice boomed. "We were all young once. Leave them alone!"

Noah showed Riley the way to the bathroom. "Sorry about that. We'll be the talk of the town now."

Riley shrugged. "Let them talk." She wrapped her free hand around his neck and pulled his mouth to hers. When she moved away, she winked at him before slipping into the bathroom and closing the door behind her.

Noah stumbled to the spare room, which had finally been set up for him, and collapsed on the bed. What was he doing? Riley was not the sort of girl he should fall for. She was too free-spirited and spontaneous for him, not to mention the very dangerous job she did and how much time she spent travelling for it. If they were to start a relationship, he could just see himself spending most nights alone, waiting for her to call and tell him all the exciting things she had done and seen.

Muster pilots had a high accident and death rate. What if she had one and was badly injured? What if she died? They didn't call them sky cowboys for nothing.

He groaned in frustration, his blood still on fire from her kiss. He wanted her so much. Maybe it would be worth it. Maybe he could steel his heart and just have a fling.

What was the saying? In it for a good time, not a long time? He couldn't do that though. Could he?

She found him there a few minutes later. He drank in the sight of her cleaned and refreshed. She sat next to him on the bed. "Give me your mobile."

He pulled it from his pocket and unlocked it before handing it to Riley. She pressed the screen a few times before handing it back. "You have my number now."

He looked at the screen, memorising the digits before sending her a message.

She opened her mobile and laughed when she saw the string of emojis.

"And now you have mine." He said.

She smiled back at him and his hand curled around the back of her neck, pulling her to him. Their lips met, her's so soft and so sweet against his. He revelled in the taste of her mouth and the way her body swayed against him, closer, all heat and warm curves. He wanted so much more from her, but this was not the time. Noah forced his mouth from Riley's and pressed his forehead against hers. He held it there, catching his breath and enjoying the feel of her rapid, excited breaths on his skin.

"We should go join the others." He said, then smiled when she made a little moan of protest.

He stood and held out his hand for her to take. She paused for a moment before accepting his chivalry. As he helped her up, he used just a little bit more force than required so she fell into his arms.

This time he made sure their kiss was both tender and controlled, even if a voice inside his head said he was already well on the way of risking his heart.

CHAPTER 13

Riley pulled the ute up in a dust cloud outside
Arabella Plains. It had been three long, frus-
trating days since the wedding, and she felt tied up in
knots and lust, counting down the minutes until she could
get Noah McGuire undressed.

They had been calling and texting each other non-stop
since she had returned to Dylan's property. Darcy and
Meghan had left for their honeymoon, and Noah was
alone on their station.

After hurrying from the driver's seat, Riley pulled out
the bags of groceries he had asked her to pick up on her
way through town. Looking around, she was disappointed he wasn't there waiting for her. Maybe he wasn't
as excited for their sexcapades to start as she was. She had
been imagining everything in fine detail, her plan of how
she would seduce him prepared in finite detail.

In the kitchen, she quickly put the groceries away and
washed her hands before she went back outside to find

him. It was after five, and the sun would start setting soon.

She found him in the arena, astride a sweaty brown stockhorse. He was trotting it around in large circles, rising and falling in time to its stride. Riley wet her dry lips.

He looked over at her and smiled, showing off his dark-haired handsomeness, sparkling blue eyes, and straight teeth. He hadn't shaved today, leaving his jaw sexily stubble-roughened. Worse, he was wearing a pair of jeans that clung to his thighs and showed off his long legs. As for the rolled-up sleeves of his shirt, on anyone else it looked agricultural and competent. Noah made it both those things and sexy as hell.

The rumblings worsened. Dammit.

She continued to regard him steadily as he finished another loping circuit before reining in the horse in front of her.

He moved his arm to glance at his watch. "That time already?"

Needing a distraction, Riley put her arm through the wooden fence railings and patted the horse's soft nose. She was rewarded with a gentle snort. She had forgotten how much she loved horses—their horsey smell and soft fur.

With the ease and fluidity of a man who had done this his whole life, Noah slid his way down the horse's back before landing softly on the firm dirt of the arena.

"Fancy a ride?" he offered with an evocative wink.

Her mind trailed off into the dirty fantasies she had spent the last few days conjuring. Her cheeks heat with anticipation before realising he meant the horse.

All thoughts of her well-planned seduction disappeared as she climbed the fence and took the reins of the magnificent animal. She ignored Noah's proffered hands, ready to help her onto the giant horse. Instead, she easily lifted herself into the saddle.

She let the long reins thread through her fingers. The horse was sensitive to her gentle squeezes and settled into a swaying walk. She leaned forward, urging him faster. The horse obliged, flattening his ears and putting on a turn of speed that had Riley releasing a whoop that was immediately whipped away into the wind behind her. She circled the arena several times, her attention solely on the horse and the exhilaration the ride brought her.

"Okay, buddy," she said, dropping her weight back into the saddle and easing him to a trot. The horse shook its head and snatched at the bit, nostrils flaring as he sucked in air. She stroked a hand down the dark streak of his neck, sweat soaked through his coat. It was exciting to be that free, that fast. It was like that when she was in the air. Nothing else mattered. She was in control and capable.

Riley pulled the horse up to a halt at the gates where Noah waited, his hands on his slender hips, a surprised smile on that gorgeous face.

"You never cease to surprise me." He took the reins as she dismounted.

"If I didn't fly helicopters, I'd happily spend my days in the saddle." She stroked the horse's neck.

"Let's rinse him off and go get some food. I'm famished," Noah said and led the way to the hose.

The pair worked side by side, chatting about horses and farm life as they unsaddled and washed their horses. After dishing out the feed and completing the other evening chores, they slowly headed back to the house. She may have imagined it, but she could have sworn Noah's hand was continually knocking against hers as they walked.

They paused at the door of the house to heave off their boots, and Noah eased the sliding glass door open. At the kitchen sink, they washed their hands and went about preparing dinner.

It had been a long time since she had cooked a proper meal and even longer since she had prepared one with a man's help. Especially a man she liked as much as Noah McGuire. It was as if they had done it a million times before. Laughing and joking, they worked around each other readying salad, meat, and potatoes. Before she knew it, they were sitting at the table, digging into their food.

Noah leaned back from the table and sighed content-edly; his plate clean. Riley stabbed her last piece of steak and piled it with the remaining potato, mopped up the juice and put it in her mouth. Still chewing, she crossed her cutlery and turned her gaze to Noah. He looked at her in awe, like she was some secret to be revealed. His gaze flickered to her mouth and self-consciously, she dabbed at it, expecting to find juice seeping from her lips.

His hand shot out and clenched her wrist. "I love your mouth. So sensual."

Her heartbeat shot through the roof and she involun-tarily swallowed too big a chunk of meat, coughing as it went down. Noah let go of her hand so she could sip her water. When her coughing fit was over, Noah took her hand again in his and pressed a kiss to her palm. Riley's skin began to goose pimple with anticipation.

"You are so beautiful."

Riley's natural reaction to compliments was to argue or brush them off. But when Noah said it, she could tell he wanted nothing in return. He was honest, simply stating the truth as he saw it.

Instead of replying to his compliment, she leaned in and brushed her lips against his. His free hand wound into the hair at the base of her neck, pulling her closer to him. The kiss deepened. Little moans formed on the back of Riley's throat as the connection turned desperate. Noah drew back briefly to regard her with wonder.

"Riley." His voice was husky with need. She kissed him again, even harder this time. They rose together, continuing to kiss as Noah steered her backwards towards his bedroom. One hand slid to her hip and found its way inside her top. Riley did the same with him, rejoicing in the strength and warmth of his belly, and every delicious inch of him. His fingers reached the underside of her breast, scrambling her brain. His rough hands pushed her bra up and cupped her. By the time he lowered her onto the bed, they were both panting hard with desire and desperation. This was unlike anything she had ever experienced. The heart-wrenching need to have him was almost more than she could bear, and judging from the way he was acting, he felt the same way about her.

She arched her back as Noah kissed his way down her neck and scraped his teeth over the skin at the hollow of her collarbone. Her T-shirt and bra were quickly discarded in the urgency and heat of the moment. His mouth and warm breath were all over her, sucking, nibbling, and discovering every inch of her tingling body.

Placing her hands on his chest, she gently pushed him onto his back. Wide-eyed, he looked at her, and she grinned mischievously back at him before unbuttoning his shirt and jeans. Then, with nimble fingers, she removed his underwear and socks until he was left naked for her pleasure. She hovered over him, memorising every curve and muscle of his magnificent body. She shimmied out of her jeans and then placed her hands on his feet, gently moving upwards over his knees, his hips, his chest, and his shoulders. She stopped to kiss his mouth before moving back again, downwards this time. She kissed her way over his heart and navel and beyond. She savoured the taste and feel of him in her hands and mouth as he groaned and shifted under her.

"Riley." The urgency in his voice had her finally releasing him and searching out his eyes. His hands found her hips and flipped her onto her back. Pulling her to the edge of the bed, he knelt, positioning himself between her thighs. It didn't take long before his fingers and tongue brought her over the edge with expert flicks, sucks, and licks. As her orgasm rolled through her in delightful quivers, he made his way back onto the bed and stroked her breasts.

She turned to him and placed her hand on his cheek, her thumb rubbing over his damp swollen lips.

"What are you doing to me?" she murmured, then kissed him deeply. She pulled him onto her, her hot body pressing against his as she urgently tried to get as close to him as possible.

He paused briefly, holding his weight over her with one hand while his other retrieved a foil packet from the bedside table. He opened it with his teeth before rolling the condom on himself. A second before he entered her their eyes locked on each other, and they didn't lose the connection until they were both writhing with pleasure at the height of ecstasy.

Temporarily sated, Riley snuggled her bum close against his hips. He splayed his fingers over her stomach, pulling her against him.

Knowing she was safe and secure in his embrace, she closed her eyes and fell asleep.

Bacon crackled, sending wafts of its pungent smell around the room. Dressed only in boxer briefs, Noah stood far enough away from the spitting pan to avoid getting hurt. If only it was so easy to protect his heart.

Being with Riley was amazing and felt so right. It was easy for him to imagine waking up with her day after day. Cooking together every evening. Making love with her every night.

And what a night it had been. Riley made him feel things he had never experienced before. Now that he had sampled her, how would he ever let her go?

Warm hands encircled his hips, and Riley's naked body pressed against his back. He hardened at her touch. Would he ever stop wanting her like this?

She pressed delicate kisses over his shoulder blades and down his spine, her hands exploring over his stomach.

"Good morning." He practically groaned. "I hope you're hungry."

She reached up and nibbled on his ear. "I'm absolutely ravenous."

Unable to resist Riley's flirtation anymore he spun around to face her. Her eyes were dark and sultry, her full lips bent up at the edges in a mischievous, seductive way.

He captured her mouth and kissed her deeply, hungrily. He lifted her up, and she wrapped her legs around his hips and pressed into him. Again, he was overcome by wanting her, needing her. When he was with her, he could shut off the world. Forget about the past, the pain, and focus just on her and the pleasure they brought each other. He wanted to cocoon them in their own little world. Just the two of them, forever.

Bacon popped behind him and Noah dragged his mouth from Riley's sweetness to turn the burner off.

"Hm, that smells good," she said peeking over his shoulder.

He inhaled her musky scent. "So do you." He nuzzled her neck then lowered her to the floor. She gave him a sexy grin before stepping out of his arms.

Noah finished preparing breakfast, although his appetite craved more of Riley than the food he was cooking.

As he dished the food onto two plates, Riley poured tea and set the table. It was oddly routine and ordinary.

But comfortable. There was no morning-after awkwardness between them.

They lingered over breakfast, Noah taking every opportunity to touch, kiss, and caress Riley, hoping his actions would speak for him, but also unable to resist the allure of her. He wanted to ask her if she felt it too, this connection between them. But fear stopped him from forming the words. What if she said no? What if it really was all in his head?

When the food was eaten and the dishes done, Riley leisurely collected her belongings, the keys jangling from her hands. Awkwardly, Noah stood in front of her, desperately wanting to kiss her and suggest another date. Hoping like hell this wasn't a one-time thing.

He thought he saw something cross over her face, but she quickly masked it with a playful smile.

"Last night was great." She wound her free hand behind his neck and pulled him towards her for a kiss which left him aching again.

"Next time you're free, you should come back. We could take some of the horses out again." He heard the hope in his voice and inwardly cringed. He didn't mean to sound so desperate.

Riley carefully moved out of his embrace and turned serious eyes on him. "Noah, I'm not looking for anything serious or long-term. I live my life day-to-day and go wherever there's a job for me."

His stomach sank. "Yeah, I know. I just thought that while you're here and I'm here, we might as well enjoy each other's company." He knew he was walking a tight rope. He should end it now while it wouldn't hurt too much. But the need to be with her, to take whatever he could, was greater than his fear of being hurt.

She raised an eyebrow. "I like spending time with you, Noah. You're a great guy. I'm happy to keep this casual as long as you are, too."

Noah didn't trust his voice, so instead, he pulled her close and kissed her fiercely. When he broke away, she had a somewhat breathless look about her. He watched as she swallowed hard.

He couldn't stop a smile curling on his lips. Riley was staring straight back at him and there it was again. The heat of connection sparking between them, inexplicable. Undeniable.

"You're welcome here anytime."

She grinned at him before opening the door. "See you later, cowboy." She blew him a kiss and left him alone to ponder when or if he would ever see her again.

CHAPTER 14

*R*iley returned to Arabella Plains two days later.

Noah hadn't been able to wait more than a few hours after she had left before messaging her. She had replied with just as much enthusiasm.

She arrived just after midday to the yapping welcome of dogs. He watched as she climbed out of Dylan's ute, the wind whipping glossy brown strands of her hair across her face.

Noah strode out to greet her, bringing her against him as soon as she was within reach.

"Hi," he said into her hair.

She grinned as though she could read his thoughts and knew just what he wanted to do to her. "Hello, you."

He moved his hands to frame her face and his mouth found hers. Her lips parted, her fingers gripped the back of his neck, and there was nothing but urgency, heat, and need between them.

He lifted her into his arms, and she wrapped her long legs around his waist.

"What about my bag?" She chuckled as he started for the house.

"We'll get it later," he replied.

Once inside, he laid her down on the bed and their gazes met. He'd never seen her eyes look a more brilliant chocolate brown or appear so luminous. He kissed her again and lost himself in the beauty and warmth of the only woman he'd ever want.

He stood long enough to pull his T-shirt over his head and let it fall to the floor. He spotted her watching him, her lips parted and eyes hooded. He took his time unbuttoning his jeans and slowly sliding them off. "Like what you see?" he asked.

She nodded as she took in every inch of him. "Very much."

He climbed onto the bed next to her and started unbuttoning her shirt, tugging it open to reveal her bra and bare midriff. "I like what I see too."

He straddled her then and placed soft kisses over her skin before flicking his tongue around her belly button. She moaned loudly, sounding so lost in pleasure, it spurred him on. All he could think about was getting her clothes off so he could make her lose her mind entirely. Unzipping the fly of her jeans, he started peeling them past her hips. Her shirt and underwear quickly joined the growing heap of clothes on the floor.

He opened her thighs and settled his face between them, his world revolving only around her delicate flesh, her musky scent, and the uncontrollable trembling of her thighs as he gave her pleasure. Her hips lifted off the bed and she shuddered into a loud, convulsive climax.

She cried out his name as he moved up her still-shaking body, kissing her breasts and swirling his tongue over the dark peaks.

She curled her fingers through his hair and he answered by capturing her mouth in a kiss and pressing his body against hers so she could feel exactly how much he wanted her.

After grabbing a condom from the bedside table, he tore it open then reached down between them to roll it on.

"I want you so bad," Riley said, wrapping her legs around his hips.

Noah moved slowly, pushing inside her, trying to savour every sensation as pleasure spread through him. Riley's hands clutched at his butt, encouraging him deeper, faster. The noises she made, the thrashing of her hips, had him coming with her, pleasure gripping him as he held himself deep inside, his face pressed into her neck.

As his heart rate slowed, he rolled off her and she curled against him. She was so fiercely independent, so determined, he hadn't figured her to be a spooner. And yet there was nothing stand-offish about the way she was plastered to the side of his body: her head on his chest, her arm around his waist, one slim leg tangled with his.

"How's it going at Dylan's?" he asked as he stroked an idle finger up and down her arm.

She sighed before speaking. "Fine. He can't afford to pay me, so I told him I'd be happy to work for free board."

"Really?" He shifted so he could see her face better.

"Beats going back to Longreach and twiddling my thumbs."

"You could stay here," he said, choosing his words carefully. "I could pay you from my own account. I'll be claiming my inheritance soon."

Riley stretched out her hand and ran her fingertips along his jaw. "That's sweet, but I think Dylan needs me more. Besides, he's letting me work my own hours, which means I can come visit you whenever I want."

She rubbed her leg suggestively up his, sending thrills of awareness prickling over his skin.

He pulled her on top of him, causing her to gasp in surprise. She sat on his belly, her hands on either side of his head. Columns of brown hair fell against his chest. He raised a hand to touch its silkiness. *So beautiful.*

"Noah." Her voice was husky with desire. His heart gave a strange little squeeze at the way she said his name. As though it was special to her. As though it meant something.

Then she was touching him, kissing him, and his brain turned to mush and all he could think about was how good it felt being with Riley. He would take as much or as little time as she gave him and not think about the heart-break that probably awaited him when it was over.

He wasn't going to miss out on being with the most exciting, sexy, challenging woman he'd ever met simply because he was scared.

∾

"I promised you a ride," Noah said later as he tugged on his jeans.

Riley stretched her toes as she devoured every magnificent, muscled inch of him, from the tips of his sun-lightened hair to his toned calves below. "Haven't we done enough riding for one day?" She raised her eyebrows in a suggestive fashion.

Smiling, he strode to the bed, grabbed her feet with his hands, and pulled her towards him. He picked her up, pressing her naked body against his.

Where did this take-charge attitude come from? She liked it. A lot.

He looked at her through his long lashes. "Am I working you too hard? Worried you won't be able to walk tomorrow?"

Heat crept up Riley's face and before she could think of something smart-arsed to say back, he was ducking his head to find her mouth. His lips were soft but firm on hers, and she gave an involuntary little moan. He took it as encouragement, his tongue tracing the seam of her lips, and when she opened to him, his groan echoed hers as his tongue swept into her mouth.

Her hands found his shoulders, her fingers digging into the muscles there as he continued his journey south, kissing the gentle rise of her collarbone and finding that sensitive spot on her neck. It was lucky he was holding her up as her knees started to weaken.

Then, without warning, he stopped and held her at arm's length. "Sorry. I didn't mean to hurt you." His brows furrowed in apology and there was a haunted look in his eyes.

She placed a soft kiss against his lips. "You didn't hurt me. I'm not that fragile."

"Come on. I promised you a horse ride and I always deliver on my promises."

"Maybe next time I can take you back up in my helicopter and we can see just what your limits are," she said before reaching for her clothes.

He turned to watch her dress. "With you, babe, I'm up for anything."

Riley grinned and couldn't help but feel like she'd just won the lottery.

After dressing, Riley followed Noah to the kitchen where he opened the fridge and pulled out a bag of carrots. "For the horses," he said with a coy smile.

Fresh country smells—cow and horse manure, eucalypt, and dusty soil—scented the air, and Riley breathed it all in as they walked to the horse yard. Ahead of them, the wind blew up whirly-whirlies of dust, reminding them they were still in the deep despair of drought. As if they could forget. This drought would remain firmly etched in every grazier's memory for the rest of their lives.

The horses came into sight, separated into groups of four, their paddocks marked by white electric tape slung between metal posts. Many raised curious gazes as they no doubt smelled the humans approaching. A foal, standing close to its mother, let out a warning whinny.

"I forgot how many Darcy owned," Riley said as she studied the animals. More than twenty roamed happily, mostly stock and quarter horses, but she also spotted a palomino and the familiar appaloosa in the mix.

"I'm sure they'd take more if they could," Noah said as he stopped to turn off the fence. "People keep calling, asking if he can take any extras. There's no feed for the cattle, let alone the horses, so they're just starving."

"It's the same in Longreach," Riley said. "And most places I've been in western Queensland."

"Yep." He let the word hang heavy in the air.

Noah led Riley to a paddock and stopped next to a picket. Rustling the bag of carrots made the animals stop and eye him curiously, and it wasn't long before a graceful black animal wandered over.

"Jasper." Riley smiled when Darcy's prized horse approached. She would know him anywhere with his noble nose, massive shoulders, and muscled rump. Even from a distance she could sense the horse's exceptional talent.

He stopped in front of them and looked her right in the face with calm, intelligent eyes.

Noah handed her a carrot and Jasper bit a chunk off the end, working his jaw as he chewed. Saliva bubbled and drooled from his mouth.

Other horses meandered over for their own treats and Noah greeted them all by name before feeding them.

They moved between paddocks until each horse had devoured a carrot then Noah turned to Riley. "How confident of a rider are you?"

"I think I've proved that I can handle myself on more than just a gentle plodder," she replied.

He pointed to a familiar chestnut with a white blaze on its nose. "Shadow needs some exercise."

Riley smiled as she recognised Meghan's horse—the one she had saddled up that first day of the muster. "Yeah, Shadow and I are good mates."

They found lead ropes in the tack shed and Riley clipped one to Shadow's halter as she nattered to the mare and led her to a pen for saddling. Noah returned a moment later with Jasper.

"Darcy alright with you riding his best campdrafting horse?" She quirked an eyebrow. She had watched Darcy ride at campdrafts and knew Jasper was something special, but also a handful if he was in a mood.

"I have to ride him every day. It's in the job description," Noah said, looping the rope on the post and reaching for a brush.

Riley followed suit, getting another one and brushing the dust from Shadow's withers. "So that's what you get to do all day?

"Look after and ride the horses and top up the cottonseed feeder. That's pretty much it," he replied. "None of the mares are pregnant at the moment and the foal is doing just fine."

Riley paused in her brushing and looked out at the flat, sun-bleached paddocks. "Sounds like a nice way to spend your time."

Noah watched her. "Could you do it? Find a property and run some animals for a living?"

She crinkled her nose. "Full time? Nah, I'd get itchy feet." She thought about all the places her job took her and all the people she met along the way. She loved her lifestyle.

"So, you won't settle down and put down roots?" She noted the hope in his voice and it tugged at her heart.

"I'm not ready yet. Maybe one day. Then again, who knows what the future holds." Riley tried to make her voice light and nonchalant. She had never promised Noah anything; she'd been honest about what she could offer. Hopefully he wasn't letting his feelings get out of hand. God knew she was having to battle her own.

Instead of prodding her with more questions, Noah turned to Jasper and buffed his head with medal-polishing enthusiasm, before sneaking him another chunk of carrot from his pocket.

They found the right-sized saddles and bridles in the tack room, and before long, their horses were ready for their ride.

After swinging into the saddle, Riley settled herself on Shadow's back before readjusting her hat. Between the humidity and the afternoon sun, she was working up quite the sweat. She could feel beads of it dripping down her spine.

Noah mounted Jasper and looked at her. "Ready?"

She nodded and followed him as he navigated the dirt track towards the shade of some old gum trees.

"How is it being back in Queensland?" she asked, pulling up beside him. "Are you getting on with your mum and Lachie okay?"

He blew out a sigh. "Yeah, we all had a bit of a heart-to-heart the night before the wedding."

She glanced sideways at him. "Want to talk about it?"

He tilted his hat lower, so it shaded his eyes. "I knew my father was a bastard. Now Lachie knows it too."

"What did he do?" Her heart was beating wildly in her chest. What had Noah gone through? What had caused him to be so submissive?

"I told you about how violent my Dad was to me." His mouth thinned and anger tinged his voice. "I knew he hit Mum sometimes, but I didn't know the full story."

Riley took a steadying breath and continued walking the horse next to him, knowing it would be easier for him to talk if they kept moving.

"What else did he do?"

Noah didn't answer right away which only made his reply that much more powerful when he answered. "He raped her. That's when I was conceived."

"The son of a bitch," she replied. He had done that to Harriet—Harriet who was nothing but kind and compassionate to everyone she met. Under that façade was a woman who had suffered the brutality of an abusive husband for years. It was unthinkable. Devasting. Riley's heart broke for the woman.

"It was the booze. That's what Mum said changed him," Noah said.

"Is that why you don't drink?" She trembled, feeling a deep need to ease his pain.

He nodded and gave a tight smile. "Now Lachie knows what Dad was like, he said he wants to stop drinking. He doesn't want to end up like him either."

"That's very smart of him. But, he'll need help. Sobriety is a day-to-day struggle," she said with a renewed fondness for Noah's brother.

"You sound like you know about it."

Riley nodded. "I have a friend who's gone through it with drugs and alcohol. He's relapsed twice." She thought of Grant's best friend who had wasted his early twenties drinking and popping pills. Ice had made it to the outback in the early nineteen-nineties and it had torn families apart.

Noah pulled his horse up at a clearing and dismounted. Riley followed suit, surprised to see a narrow creek still flowing despite the water shortage. Noah picked up some small stones from the riverbed and tossed them, one by one into the water.

He seemed calmer when he turned to her. "Sorry. You didn't need to hear about our family drama."

She walked towards him and ran her hand over his arm. "Thank you for telling me. I want to help. If I can."

He captured her hand in his and she gazed at the hand cradling hers. His fingers were long, tapering to rough tips, his skin warm and slightly callused. A worker's hands. Capable hands. Hands you could place your trust into.

She looked back at his face. *So handsome.* His gaze softened, causing her heart to do a slow flip-flop. She caught the edge of a crooked smile before he bent to kiss her. Whatever his deepest feelings, the kiss burned with intensity, his hands cradling her face like she was fragile and precious. Her own were fisted into his shirt, dragging him nearer.

Her thoughts faded as the pressure increased and desire exploded.

Then it was over and he was pulling away and casting

an assessing eye at the late afternoon sun. "We should get back. Still got to rug up and feed the horses."

She took a steadying breath and willed her pulse to slow before getting up in the saddle.

They turned and rode back the way they had come. She made sure the conversation remained light and on safer topics. They talked about the muster and it was obvious from his tone that Noah had loved it. That despite everything he had been through, everything he had done, he remained a simple cowboy who liked nothing better than to trail cattle on a good horse, the sun warm on his shoulders.

While she was a pilot—a bird who needed to fly. There was nothing in between them except the cloudless blue sky.

The sky had turned indigo by the time they reached the stables, the horizon a pale-gold glow of rapidly fading sun. The mood lighter, they hosed down their horses before rugging them up for the night.

Noah inhaled the smells of leather, horse, and hay—smells he loved. He watched Riley wrap her arms around Shadow's neck and snuggle against her. The horse wickered gently at her affection. Riley ruffled her forelock and kissed her cheek. 'You're a good girl. I hope I haven't worn you out, hmm?'

Shadow blinked huge brown eyes and bunted against her, making Riley laugh.

Noah watched her for a few minutes longer, a strange,

full sensation building in his chest. He'd been hollow for so long that it was a weird feeling, and too much for his screwed-up head to process.

Being with Riley made him dissatisfied with the lonely life he'd led, made him want more.

He wanted the soulmate love Darcy had with Meghan.

He had always been short of confidence, pounded by guilt and grief and shame from his past. But in a short time with Riley, he could feel his self-esteem strengthening, like he was becoming a proper man again.

If he hadn't already loved her for a million other reasons, he would have loved her for that alone.

She let go of the animal and sighed happily, her hands on her hips as she turned to look at him.

Unable to voice his feelings for her, he closed the remaining distance between them, pulling her close. And as her soft lips parted, all he could think about was dipping his head and kissing her to prove to himself it was enough just to be with her right now. That the future didn't matter.

The seconds stretched, the only sound between them the accelerated rush of their breathing.

It was the horses' hungry neighing that had them finally break apart.

Riley looked up at him, her hands still curled around his neck. "Let's get this lot fed, then we can go back to the house ..." Mischief lightened her eyes as she let the implication of her words hang heavy in the air.

He swallowed hard and slid his hands into his jeans pockets, not to warm them but to stop himself from tugging her close.

"The hay's this way," he said, nodding to a shed next to the stable. She walked in front and while she wasn't watching, he took a couple of steadying breaths. It really wasn't fair that a woman could have this much pull on a man.

Especially when he was trying so hard to shield his heart.

CHAPTER 15

*T*he next two weeks passed by like a dream with Riley either flying to Arabella Plains or making the long drive every few days, just so they could spend a night together.

Noah kept himself busy when she wasn't there, trying hard not to think about her and all the things he still wanted to do to her. The nights they spent together were filled with mind-blowing sex and tender caresses. Whenever Noah felt his emotions build, he would shove them down, knowing that Riley had no intention of forming a serious relationship with him or any man. Perhaps she just needed time. Surely she would see how good they were together, and she'd change her mind.

He tried not to think about what he'd do when his house-sitting job was over, and his brother and new sister-in-law came back. He was content with the current situation.

He spoke to Lachie and Harriet most evenings and felt optimistic about their strengthening bond. Lachie had even hinted about a position being available for him on Brigadier Station whenever he was ready.

Everything was going well for the first time in a long time. Noah was truly happy.

He and Riley were lounging in bed one evening when the call came in. They'd just had a sweaty sex session to rival the hardest gym workout, and Noah was tracing lazy fingers over her perfect mounds when her mobile phone started buzzing on the bedside table. With a groan, she moved from his reach and answered the call.

"Hey, Grant," she said cheerily, a smile on her face.

He watched her murmur and nod as she listened to her cousin. "No problem. I'll leave tomorrow. Okay, see you then."

She ended the call and put the phone back down before snuggling into Noah's side as if nothing had happened.

He waited for her to tell him what the conversation had been about, but when she stayed silent, his heart flip-flopped. "How's your cousin?"

"He's good. There's a job for me in Cloncurry. I'll only be gone a couple of days though," she said, stroking her fingertips over his sensitive inner arm.

As much as he was enjoying her caress, a cold shiver of dread came over him. He raised himself on his forearm so he could look into her eyes. "Is it a mustering job?"

"Yeah, the bank has foreclosed and wants to ship what's left of the cattle to Asia ASAP. I'm meeting Grant up there tomorrow afternoon."

"Grant can't do it alone?"

She stiffened then slid out from under him to sit up,

pulling the sheets around her chest. "Usually I would do it alone."

"Then why is Grant going too?" He sensed there was more to the story that she wasn't telling him.

"He's not busy, so he thought he'd come give me a hand. We do that sometimes." She had her hackles raised now. "Stop asking me so many questions. This is my job." She turned from him and climbed out of bed, gathering the clothes that had been strewn all over the room.

Noah took a steadying breath. "Riley, I'm sorry." He followed her and reached out his arms. She looked into his eyes. Her body was rigid, but at least she wasn't fighting him. "I just have a bad feeling about this one. I can't explain it."

"I do this all the time. You don't have to worry about me," she insisted.

He raked his hand through his hair. "I know. I can't help it."

She rolled her eyes. "This is why I don't date. I hate when people tell me what to do. Don't try to control me."

He held his arms up in submission. "I don't want to control you. I want to be with you. I want you to be safe." He stood there, naked and more vulnerable than he had ever been in his life. The words "I love you" were on the tip of his tongue, and he was as surprised to find them there as she would have been if he'd had the guts to say them.

But he wouldn't say them. He couldn't.

Instead, he cupped her face in his hands and kissed her. It was intense, brief, and laden with meaning. Exactly the way he wanted it to be.

She sank into him, her supple body against his hard one. "I'll be fine. You won't even know I'm gone," she murmured.

He wanted to say more, to ask her to promise to be safe, to promise to come back, but he understood she didn't want to hear that. And he didn't want to sound like an oversensitive, needy child. She wanted him to trust her and he did. He knew she had the knowledge and experience to do this job, no matter what dangers may arise.

After dinner, they shared another night together. This time, the lovemaking was slow and gentle. He made sure she was pleasured and that it was a night they would both remember no matter what.

When she fell asleep in his arms, he watched her for a long time. The full extent of his feelings for her rose, forced their way to the surface. Love swelled in him as he watched her chest rise and fall, the little purring noises she made as she slept, the fluttering of her long eyelashes.

He didn't want to lose her, so he would have to come up with a plan. A way to show her that they could work, that they could have a successful, trusting relationship. He didn't know how but he would think of something. He finally fell asleep, exhausted from worry.

In the morning, he reached for her and found only an empty space where she had been. He sat up in bed, listening for any movements in the house.

There were none. She was gone.

CHAPTER 16

*A*s she flew over the parched brown Queensland outback, Riley let her thoughts linger on Noah and their conversation the night before. She hadn't wanted to sneak out this morning, but she also hadn't wanted to argue with him, especially not when she was leaving for a job. She didn't like any distractions when she was flying. Heli-mustering required absolute concentration and attention to detail. Accidents occurred when pilots got distracted.

She should never have started seeing Noah. She had thought they could keep it casual, just great sex and a good time, but it had been too easy to let it morph into something more. Before she knew it, they were playing house.

Last night, she had seen it in his eyes; he was falling for her. If she was honest with herself, she felt more than just friendship for him too. Damn, why had she let this happen?

She shouldn't go back after this job. She should return

to Longreach and try to forget about Noah McGuire. Dylan would be disappointed, but she had managed to get a lot accomplished on his property.

Leaving would be the smart thing to do. But she loved being with Noah. She loved the way he made her feel: safe, secure, and loved. And he was one of the good ones. Honest, protective, and down to earth. If she was ever going to settle down with anyone, Noah McGuire would be her best choice.

She shook her head as the airstrip come into view. Grant's familiar yellow Robinson R22 was already parked with its blades tied down as she came to land a few metres away from it. She turned off the engine and climbed out, spotting him waiting for her.

"Good to see you," he said, nodding a greeting. "How's everything going?"

She shrugged nonchalantly. "Fine. How about you?"

"Everything is going great. Actually, I have some news." His eyes were sparkling with excitement, and the huge smile on his face was something she had never seen before.

"Spit it out."

"Andrea is pregnant. I'm going to be a dad."

She took a beat to process the news before flinging her arms around him and squeezing him. "Congratulations. How far along is she?"

"Twelve weeks. That's why I'm here; I wanted to tell you in person that I've decided this will be my last flight for a while. I'm going to retire from flying and just run the business and let you do all the hard work."

"Pretty much runs like that now." She grinned at him,

thrilled that her cousin had found happiness and love with such a wonderful woman, and would soon have children of his own. It was incredible news and she was so happy for them. But it also stirred feelings in her and yearnings she hadn't thought she had.

"Well, it's official now. If that's okay with you?" His grin was wide. Happiness was evident on every feature of his face.

"Of course it is, and let's face it: I'm the better pilot anyway."

"I see you're still as arrogant as always. Did anything end up happening with your friend's brother?"

She shot him an it's-none-of-your-business look before busying herself tying down the blades and doing her post-flight inspection. Knowing her cousin, he would grill her for information later. But right now, she needed a bit of time to think about Noah and decide if there was a place for him in her future.

Getting nose-to-nose with stragglers was just a part of the job for a cowboy, whether on a horse, or a quad bike, or in a helicopter. Riley was constantly dipping and diving to drive the cattle home. Continually flying in what pilots called the 'dead man's zone'—flying low and flying slow.

She levelled the helicopter a metre above the ground, and the cattle in front of her shuffled forward before breaking into a run, moving exactly where she needed them to go. As she gained height, she scoured the land below for any stragglers.

She glanced over at Grant's yellow chopper, busy doing the same techniques to flush them out. The small, manoeuvrable helicopter flew low, mere feet above the ground.

He had taught her the moves he was using now. From him, she had learnt about timing and how to feel the controls through her feet. He had also explained to her how important cow sense was. Mustering in a helicopter wasn't so different from mustering on horseback; she still needed to have an idea of what the animals were going to do and see it coming before they acted on it.

Grant had been fortunate enough to be raised on a cattle station, so when Riley had showed interest, he'd invited her along on musters. From then on, she had spent all her spare time learning about cattle and working with them. She was confident in her abilities on the ground and in the sky. With more than two thousand hours of low-flying experience, she had exceptional knowledge of the cattle and could anticipate where they might play up and give her trouble. She knew exactly what sort of move would be able to turn them.

She continued to push the mob in the direction of the yards, constantly keeping an eye out for stragglers or hiding places that might be concealing the dust-coloured beasts.

She loved it up here; she really did. She couldn't let Noah take this away from her. No one could take this away from her. Grant was lucky that Andrea supported him and his career. She had never tried to talk him out of doing what he loved, what he had worked so hard to train for.

If Noah wanted to be in her life, he would have to understand that she would never give up flying—not for him, not for anyone.

She smiled as she thought about Grant's impending fatherhood. They would have a beautiful child with Grant's intelligence, and Andrea's good looks and sense of humour.

Riley would get to be their child's aunt. She would be able to babysit and play with the child. Reward him or her with lollies and toys. She would be the fun aunt, the person they could talk to about their love life and school. She wouldn't judge them or their decisions and she would encourage and love them no matter what.

Riley had never let herself consider motherhood. She didn't want to have a serious relationship because of her job, so there was certainly no way she wanted to have children. Risking death or injury was an occupational hazard for her, but she wouldn't inflict the risk on anyone else.

She pursed her lips together and forced her mind back to the mob in front of her. She couldn't afford to be distracted.

A sudden movement had her twisting her head just in time to see her cousin's yellow bird spinning around and around. She levelled her own helicopter and watched in horror, praying that Grant would get his under control. "Come on, Grant. You can do it."

But he was too low to the ground, and there was nowhere to go but down.

Riley screamed as his blades clipped the branches of an old gum tree. There was a loud screech of grinding metal, and it all became a blur of smoke, dust, and flames.

Her heart pounding madly in her chest, Riley radioed in the emergency to the guys on the ground and landed as close to the accident site as she could.

She spotted him in the mangled cockpit, the skids brown below it. She didn't hesitate. Using all her strength, she managed to pull the flimsy door open. She grabbed the pocket knife from her belt, thankful she wore it in case of emergencies, and cut Grant free of his safety harness.

She dragged him away from the helicopter as flames started to lick closer to the fuel tank. No sooner had she cleared the wreck than it exploded, the smell of aviation gasoline polluting the air. Adrenaline pumped through her veins, and she turned her attention back to Grant.

First-aid knowledge was essential in her line of work, and she started CPR when she couldn't find Grant's pulse.

"Come on, come back," she muttered as she pumped his chest. "Think of Andrea. Think of your child. You can't die on me. Not out here. Not now."

She barely noticed the arrival of the men on quad bikes. Barry, the man in charge, put his fingers to Grant's neck and after a few seconds, he looked up at her. "You can stop now."

No. He couldn't be. Not her Grant—the only member of her family she had. *Oh, Grant!* She gaped at him. Her heart broke. "No."

He shook his head. "There's a pulse. You can stop CPR."

Riley groped Grant's neck and sure enough, his

blood was weakly pumping through his veins. She leaned back on her knees and surveyed the rest of his injuries. There was a nasty gash in his thigh and another on his forehead. Barry was applying pressure to his wounds.

"The Flying Doctor will be here soon." Barry's voice was calm and deep. "You did great, Riley."

She rubbed her hands over her face, wiping away the wet tears from her cheeks.

She could just make out the sound of the aeroplane above the crackling of the fire devouring the helicopter, leaving only ashes behind.

Once the plane had landed, the doctor and nurse came running to the scene, laden down with medical bags. Barry explained what had happened. Within minutes, Grant was wearing a neck brace and being loaded into the small aircraft.

"We'll know more when we get to Townsville Hospital. There's room if you want to come with us," the flight nurse explained.

Riley glanced briefly at her helicopter, unsure of how safe it would be out here in this field, the cattle job half done. What would Grant think if she left the scene and went with him. He would probably scold her later for leaving such an expensive helicopter in the middle of nowhere without even tying down the blades.

Good. All she wanted was for him to be well enough to give her a good talking to.

She nodded at the nurse and climbed in. Grant would forgive her. The helicopter could be replaced. He couldn't. She needed to be there for him now. And Andrea. She needed to call Andrea. How would she react? Especially in her current state?

Tears burned in her eyes. Riley had witnessed crashes before, but never so terrifying and never when someone she loved had been involved.

This was what Noah was worried about. Feeling useless and fearful, having a loved one hurt and not being able to do anything.

Grant wasn't out of the woods yet. The crash had been bad—the worst she'd ever seen. And just when he had so much to live for too.

As the plane took off and circled the paddock, she focused her attention on what had gone wrong. Had it been her fault? Maybe there had been a loose wire? Maybe he had clipped a bird?

There were so many possibilities and every pilot would react differently under stress.

In this line of work, there were so many ways to die.

CHAPTER 17

"Robinson R22 helicopter has crashed on a cattle station near Cloncurry," the news announcer reported on the local television station. Noah had absently turned it on when he came in after work, needing some noise in the otherwise silent house.

He slammed the fridge door shut, no longer hungry, and ran to the living room where he stood and stared at the screen. His heart pummelled in his chest. "No. Please don't let it be Riley."

"Two pilots were in the air, mustering cattle, when one of them reportedly hit a tree and crashed. The victim has serious injuries and has been transported to Townsville Base Hospital."

Noah collapsed into the closest chair, his mind whirling with possibilities. What were the odds there were more musters going on at other stations in Cloncurry today? He shook his head; even he knew the odds were low. It might not be Riley, though. Grant was flying too. The reporter never said if it was a man or woman. *Shit.*

He grabbed his mobile from his back pocket and called Riley's number, but it went straight to message bank.

He hung up and dialled Lachie. His brother always seemed to know everything that happened in the district.

Lachie answered on the second ring. "I just saw the news. Is it Riley?" His brother's voice was full of concern.

"I don't know; that's why I'm calling you." Noah brushed his hand through his hair. "How do I find out? I can't think what I should do."

"Calm down. I'll call around and see what I can learn. You just stay put and I'll call you back," Lachie said before hanging up.

Noah waited for him to call back, pacing around the house, his phone growing warm in his sweaty palm. Finally, it rang, and he pounced on the answer button.

"Noah, she's okay."

Relief flooded through Noah. "What happened? Was she there?"

Lachie took a deep breath before breaking the news. "She watched it all happen. It was her cousin, Grant. Riley called for help and stayed with him until they arrived. The hospital said she saved his life."

"Where is she?" Noah imagined the scene. It must have been so traumatic for her. "Is Grant okay?"

"She's in Townsville. She's in shock because she witnessed it all. Grant is still critical, and it doesn't look too good."

"He's the only family she has." Riley must have been so worried. "I've tried calling her, but she didn't pick up."

"Are you alright? Do you want me to come over?"

Noah didn't know what he wanted except to talk to Riley. To hear her voice and know it was true—that she was alive and in one piece.

When he didn't answer, there was a rustling noise on the phone and his mother spoke in her calm, soothing manner. "Sweetheart, are you there?"

"Mum," he whispered, gulping down the welling emotion.

"Lachie and I are leaving now. We'll come be with you soon. Stay put."

"Okay." He ended the call and stared at his phone numbly.

He tried calling Riley again, and when she still didn't answer, he sent her a text message asking her to call him. She was probably too busy with doctors and paperwork to respond. Better he leave her alone and wait for her reply.

He knew he shouldn't have let her go. He should have trusted his gut feeling. But Riley was a strong, independent woman, and nothing he had or could have said would have stopped her from going.

Would this change anything? Would she still put her life on the line to do this dangerous job?

Harriet and Lachie pulled up at Arabella Plains two hours later. Noah hugged his mother, grateful for the company and support they offered.

"Have you heard anything?" Lachie asked as Harriet put the kettle on for tea.

"She finally sent me a message a little while ago." His fingers were shaking as he opened the message on his phone and read it aloud. "Grant has been in an accident. I'm fine. I'll call you tomorrow."

"That's it?" Harriet's voice was filled with surprise.

"At least she responded, finally." Her message had eased his worry only slightly. She was withdrawing from him though. He could feel it.

"Maybe she's waiting to know the full extent of Grant's injuries." Harriet handed him a cup of milky tea and he held it between his hands, letting the warmth soothe his body.

"I could call the hospital again for an update," Lachie offered.

Harriet patted his arm in agreement. "Please do."

Lachie nodded and left the room.

Noah put his cup on the table. "I asked her not to go."

Harriet moved closer to her son and put her arms around him. "Riley is a woman who knows her own mind. No one can control her."

"I don't want to control her."

There was compassion in his mother's eyes.

"I just want to love her."

Harriet stroked his head and murmured soothingly, "I know, sweetheart."

A few minutes later, Lachie returned, grim-faced.

"Grant is in a coma. But he broke his back in the accident. Even if he wakes up, the doctors say that he'll never walk again."

Harriet gasped and pressed her hand against her mouth. Noah put his head in his hands and silently wept for Grant's family.

And for Riley.

$\mathcal{T}$he doctors called it post-traumatic shock syndrome. PTSD. Wasn't that something returning soldiers got after war? People who'd been in serious accidents?

She hadn't been involved in the accident; she had only witnessed it. But the doctors felt it necessary to prescribe her a bunch of medications that would apparently help her. The only one she did routinely take was the one to help her sleep.

Night-time was the worst. She would toss and turn, reliving the accident. Wondering if there was something she could have done differently. Sometimes she even dreamed it was her helicopter that had gone down. She was the one who had been injured and almost died.

She didn't want to be propped up by medication though or depend on it too much. If she ever wanted to fly again, she had to be sober and free of all drugs. She would get through this. Somehow.

She padded softly along the hallway to the kitchen.

Noah sat at the table, crunching through cereal as he read the local paper. He looked up at her and seemed to force a smile. He didn't look at her like he used to. Instead of desire and affection, there was only pity in his eyes.

She had returned to Arabella Plains because she'd had nowhere else to go. It had taken him driving to Townsville and physically putting her in the car for her to leave Grant's side.

The doctors were happy with his recovery. After a few days in a coma, he had woken up and was recovering well. There was nothing they could do about his spine though. While he could still move his arms and neck, he was now a paraplegic.

But what kind of a life would he have? He would never be able to fly a helicopter again or drive a car. What about when his baby was born? It would be so hard for him to help out and play with his child.

"How did you sleep?" Noah asked as she poured herself a cup of coffee. She barely ate anymore, having lost her appetite. She would nibble on the occasional piece of toast, but that was enough.

Noah was trying to help her. He had made up the guest room for her and tried to give her plenty of space. She didn't understand why he was being so accommodating. He had tried to stop her going. Did he feel guilty? Was that it?

She ignored his question and sipped on her coffee.

"There are a few horses that need exercising. We could take them for a ride? Maybe pack a picnic?" he suggested.

Riley leaned against the kitchen bench. "No thanks."

"How about we drive into town then? I have some supplies to pick up."

Again, she shook her head. She didn't want to go to town. She didn't want to be around people. People put her on edge. They wanted to talk to her and ask her questions. She didn't want to talk, especially not about the accident. She also found herself not wanting to leave the house. Staying in her pyjamas, in bed, was all she could bring herself to do these days.

Noah stood from the table and took his dishes to the sink. "It's been two weeks. I really think you need to leave the house today. We'll do whatever you want."

"I don't want to go anywhere." He still didn't understand that she didn't want him telling her what to do. She would leave the house when she was damn well ready to. She would make her own decisions. She studied his face and took a deep breath.

Silence stretched between them, thick with the weight of unspoken words. Words like 'I think you need help' from Noah. Words like 'I'm goddamn fine' from her.

She broke the stillness first. "Actually, there is something I want to do."

He looked up at her with wide, hopeful eyes.

"I want to go back to Longreach. I need to be there when Grant comes home."

Noah's expression fell. He stood and reached for her, but she pulled away from his touch. "It's going to be weeks before he's discharged."

"I know, but I should be there. I should be running the business. I still have to get my helicopter back." Her thoughts returned to the scene of the accident. The helicopter had been flown to the aero club and was safe there until she could organise its transport home. What remained of Grant's chopper was still in the paddock. The wind had probably blown it away by now.

"You're not honestly going to fly again, are you? So soon?" Noah stared at her horrified.

Riley hadn't made a decision about her future. Flying was all she knew, all she was trained for. Now she had no idea what she would do, but it was her choice to make. "I don't know. But I can't stay here."

His face softened, a yearning in his expression. "You can. It's too soon. Let me take care of you."

She raised her head at him defiantly. There was no way she would let him or anyone else take care of her. "No. Whatever we had, it's gone now. I've changed. I don't know how, but I can't be that girl I used to be anymore."

He moved towards her, and she stepped back. If he touched her, she would lose her nerve.

"We can make it work, Riley. We can have a life together."

"No, I don't want that. I never did. I want my independence. I want to be free." The words tasted bitter. It was easy enough to say them, but she didn't know if she truly meant them anymore. But she didn't want to be with a man who pitied her. Or who stayed with her out of obligation. It was best to end things now.

Noah leaned on the table. He looked like he had just been punched to the gut. "Fine. If that's how you feel."

He turned from her and left the room, taking her heart with him.

The drive into town was slow and eerily silent. There were a thousand things Noah wanted to say to Riley, but she had made her feelings clear. They had no future together. Their time was over.

As much as he hated to admit it, she was right. Everything was different now. Grant's accident had changed things. It had made Noah realise just how much he loved Riley.

She was spiralling into a well of depression and he didn't know how to help her. She didn't want it, and that just made it worse. He could only hope that when she was back in Longreach, she would have support and hopefully get the professional help the doctor had recommended.

He parked in front of the lonely bus stop on the highway. "When's it due?"

Riley glanced at her watch. "Ten minutes. Thanks for the ride." She opened her door and climbed out.

He sat, frozen in place as she grabbed her bag from the tray of the ute. His fingernails dug into the soft palm of his hand and he forced himself to get it together.

He slammed the door behind him and strode towards her. "Riley."

She spun around, eyes wide.

He put his hands on her shoulders and dragged her to him. He let his kiss do the talking, hoping to remind her of their passionate, love-filled nights.

His tension eased as her hands threaded through his hair, pulling him closer. Hope sparked where he thought it was gone forever.

Finally, he moved back and rested his forehead against hers. Her breathing was just as laboured as his.

"I love you," he whispered, needing her to know how much he cared about her.

She bit her lip and sniffed, then wrapped her arms around him, her grip desperate. He didn't think she was crying, but she was close to, which somehow made it even more heartbreaking.

A honking noise drew their attention and they turned to see the big grey bus pulling up to park in front of them.

Riley stepped out of Noah's embrace and hoisted her bag over her shoulder. "I'm sorry, Noah. I need to go."

Reluctantly, he let her leave. He thrust his hands into his jeans pockets and watched helplessly as she climbed onboard the bus, then paused to buy a ticket from the driver.

As the bus door closed, she disappeared from his sight. He searched for her in the darkly tinted windows but could only see himself reflected in the glass.

A desperate, lovesick man who had just lost the love of his life.

CHAPTER 19

*S*ix months later

"Here's Aunty Ry," Andrea cooed at her baby boy as she placed the precious bundle into Riley's waiting embrace.

Riley snuggled his warm body into the crook of her arm and started to rock gently back and forth in the chair.

Alexander Grant Sinclair was the most perfect baby ever born. His aunt might have been a little bit biased, but she was pretty sure he would win any cutest baby award. She just wanted to stare at his beautiful face and tiny fingers all day long and breathe in that sweet, milky, baby smell.

"Hey, what does a father have to do to get some time with his son?" Grant playfully complained as he rolled into the room. Riley glanced at him and noted how muscled and strong his arms had become since using the wheelchair. Although he still had his off days, he had adapted well to his new way of life.

"I'll let you two fight it out. Mummy needs a shower," Andrea said before leaning down to plant a kiss on Grant's mouth.

Grant wheeled over to Riley and gazed at his son. "God, I'm lucky," he murmured as he stroked the baby's fine brown hair.

Riley frowned at him. "You're in a wheelchair. How is that lucky?"

He gave her a genuine, grateful smile. "I'm here, aren't I? I'll get to see Alex grow up. I almost didn't get that."

"You shouldn't have been in Cloncurry at all. I could have handled it myself. You should have been here, safe."

"Stop blaming yourself, Ry." He put his hand on her elbow. "You are not to blame. I flew too close to the tree. I thought there was more space."

"It was an accident." Her voice wavered just the tiniest amount—a small ripple in the dam of her surety.

"Exactly. An accident." His tone was final. "I came so close to not being here at all. If you hadn't seen me go down and gotten me out, I would be dead now."

"But Grant ..." She motioned towards his limp, lifeless legs. "You'll never walk again. Never fly again."

"So, we make a few alterations to the car and house. I use ramps instead of stairs. It hasn't been easy, and there are still lots of adjustments to make. But, we'll get through it. I'm so happy to be alive. I thank God every day." He winked at her. "Besides, never say never."

Riley looked back at the baby and let Grant's words

sink in. There were still so many things possible for him. Disabled people were achieving amazing things every day. Yet, here she was moping about like it was the end of the world when she still had two perfectly good legs.

She let her mind drift to Noah and, instead of shutting those thoughts down like she usually did, she wondered where he was and what he was doing. She missed him so much. The feel of his body on hers and the good times they had shared. During these past six months, she had often found herself pausing over his name in her contacts, wanting to call him and hear his voice and his heart-tingling laugh.

She had left because she was unwell. But now, with regular counselling and medication, Riley was managing to get through the day without feeling sorry for herself.

The windows rattled as the deep drone of an aero-plane flying over the house caught her attention. Back when business was booming, Grant had purposely bought a house as close to the airport as he could get, so he was always close to his machines. After the accident, when she'd first come back to the house, the noise had triggered panic attacks, the sounds of the jet engines pulling forth those painful images and gut-wrenching terror. Riley would curl into a ball on the floor, her hands flat against her ears until the aircraft noise had faded.

Now she caught herself moving to the window and watching as the Cessna landed on the runway. The quiet certainty that she was over the worst filled her with hope.

She did miss flying. A manager and another pilot had been brought in to run the business in Riley and Grant's absence, but there was only so long they could afford to pay their wages.

Riley turned to Grant with sheer determination written all over her face. "I'm going to the hangar."

Grant looked up at her with wide eyes and the hint of a smile. "Good weather for it."

She strode across the room with a sense of purpose that she hadn't felt in a long time.

A few minutes later, she was unlocking the hangar doors and letting the afternoon sun stream into the shed. Her blue helicopter sat alone on the concrete floor, waiting for her.

She couldn't help but smile as she ran her fingers over the smooth shell as she circled the machine. The new pilot had obviously been taking good care of her. She was sparkling clean, and as Riley checked the oil and fluid, she noted everything was topped up and shipshape.

The fuel bowser groaned as she pumped avgas into the chopper's fuel tank. The potent smell clearing her sinuses as adrenalin pumped through her system.

Next, she attached wheels to the skids and pushed the helicopter out onto the helipad. If she focused on one activity at a time she would be fine. She had done these jobs a million times before; there was nothing to be nervous of.

With nothing left to do, Riley climbed into the cockpit. Everything was just as it should be. Just as she'd left it.

With nimble fingers, she reached out and cupped her hand around the cyclic. A pang of fear sliced through her and she jolted her hand back. Squeezing her eyes shut, she braced herself for the attack. But it didn't come. Instead, her breathing returned to normal and she felt a calmness surround her.

An image of Noah appeared in her mind, looking stupidly sexy in jeans and a blue work shirt that hugged his chest and showed off his broad shoulders and muscular arms. Lines bracketed his face and eyes, and there was an earnestness to his expression.

She would fly again. She would do it for him, for Grant, and for herself. If she could conquer this fear, she could do anything.

Including getting Noah back.

She started the engine and smiled as it purred to life. The sound of the rotors swishing above her was like music to her ears.

Ready to go, with her headset and seat belt on, she was soon lifting off the ground and flying over Grant's house. She dipped slightly as she spotted Andrea in her front yard, Alex nestled against her chest. Riley couldn't see him, but she knew Grant would be watching her from the window.

One day, when he was ready too, she would take Grant up again. She would be his wings. Hell, they could rig up a helicopter to be all hand-operated and he could fly himself. With modern technology, anything was possible.

She rose higher in the air and watched as the cars and houses grew smaller and the horizon spread wider in front of her.

The air rushed past the window as she picked up speed. She was back in the sky.

She flew as though she had never stopped, knowing with deep certainty she was right where she was meant to be. She was a bird, after all, and now that her wings were healed, nothing could keep her from taking to the sky once more.

CHAPTER 20

*R*iley circled Arabella Plains once before preparing to land on the airstrip where Darcy and Meghan were waiting for her. Excitement at seeing her friends again overshadowed any feelings of anxiety she may have felt during the trip from Longreach.

As she landed back on the familiar brown dirt of the station, emotions threatened again. She was closer to Noah now than she had been in months. Darcy, so similar in appearance to his brother, waited for her with a smile as she opened the cabin door and climbed out, the blades slowly coming to still above her.

"It's so good to see you." Meghan stepped forward and embraced her, and Riley found herself relaxing into her arms.

"You too. I'm sorry I haven't kept in touch better."

When Meghan let her go, Darcy put his arm around her shoulders and gave her a stoic man-hug. "We're really glad you called."

Riley hadn't wanted to call Noah or let him know she

was coming. What she wanted to say had to be said in person.

Darcy had let slip that Noah was working at Brigadier Station with Lachie. She had been worried he might have returned to New Zealand and left the outback again. Maybe for good this time.

Back at the house, they gathered in the garden, which was still green despite the dry and dusty heat. Riley sipped her cold beer and chatted easily with her friends. "How was your honeymoon?" They had returned soon after Grant's accident and she was ashamed she hadn't caught up with them earlier.

"It was wonderful." Meghan held Darcy's hand as they gazed into each other's eyes, so obviously in love.

As they chatted about their holiday, Riley found herself wondering if she would feel the same about Noah when she saw him. But what worried her more was if he would still feel the same about her. It had been many months, after all. He could have met someone else.

"Noah will be glad to see you," Darcy said as if reading her mind.

Riley gave him a tight smile. "Do you think so? I mean, I haven't talked to him since I left. We didn't part on good terms."

Meghan leaned forward. "That man has been pining for you. Big time."

"Really?" Hope ignited in her heart. She was risking everything coming out here, but she needed to see him and talk to him. To see if there was still something between them or if the embers of their relationship had truly gone out.

"I don't want to see either of my brothers hurt, and I hope they both find happiness like what Meghan and I have." Darcy looked at his wife for a moment before turning back to Riley. "You and Noah had something special. I honestly think you're the one for him."

Riley's eyes moistened at his touching words. Darcy believed it. Now she just had to hope Noah did too.

She just had to find the right words. How could she say all she had stored up in her heart? All the worries she had about Grant and Andrea, but everything else too? How at some point, he'd stopped being a fling and started being the man she wanted to spend her life with? How he somehow knew what she needed when she didn't know herself? How he thought he was damaged and worthless, but really, he had more strength than anyone else she knew.

Noah had made her feel safe, adored, and understood. The part of her that she'd always held back was no longer content to remain in hiding. She wanted to invest all of herself.

Hopefully he still felt the same ...

The bitter smell of diesel and oil enveloped Noah as he crouched next to the forklift and used all his energy to turn the spanner. Blasted bolt just wouldn't come off, and what should have been a quick job had already taken the better part of an hour. He wiped sweat from his forehead with his greasy hand and cursed.

It had been his decision to stay on at Brigadier Station

when Darcy and Meghan had returned. Lachie was short-handed, so Noah spent his days helping to run the family property. Their neighbours, Dylan and Maddie, were still struggling with the weight of debt they had incurred, and Lachie and Noah helped whenever they could.

"Do you think they'll sell up?" Noah had asked over dinner a few nights ago.

"I don't think they'll have much of a choice," Lachie had replied sadly. It would be a great loss to the community to see their young family forced to sell.

"Could you buy it?" Noah had ventured. "Add it on to Brigadier Station?"

"We have enough of our own problems. If I knew we were going to finally get some rain, then maybe I could, but I don't think the bank would help right now."

"How much do you need?"

"More than you got in your inheritance, little brother." Lachie had grinned affectionately.

Darcy and Lachie had both been told just how much Noah would get for holding up his end of the bargain. It was a modest amount. Enough to buy a house in the suburbs or put a deposit on a small station. Noah had sought good advice before investing it. He didn't have any plans for the future. He didn't know if he wanted to buy his own place just yet. He was still young, after all, and there was a lot of the world he hadn't seen. Hell, he had barely seen anything of Australia.

The crunch of gravel and rumble of a car engine had Noah throwing down the spanner in frustration. Lachie could fix his own damn forklift. He stood and went to confront his brother who had gone to town early that morning.

But it wasn't his brother's ute that pulled up in front of the house. It was Darcy's.

Then the door opened and instead of Darcy climbing out, it was someone else. Someone he'd never expected to see again.

Noah froze. He'd fantasised about this moment a million times, but he'd stopped believing it would ever happen. Now here she was. Flesh and blood.

She'd lost weight, but she still took his breath away. A warm breeze lifted her hair and made her pale blue shirt billow. He wanted to pinch himself to make sure he wasn't imagining her, like he had so often.

As she walked towards him all those feelings began bubbling to the surface. Feelings he had tried so hard to forget.

"Hi." Riley stood just within arm's reach, and he shoved his hands in his pockets so he wouldn't do something stupid like pull her to him and kiss her. God, he wanted to kiss her. She looked so beautiful.

"How are you?" His voice sounder rougher than he meant as he tried to steel himself.

She shrugged, never taking her eyes off his. Like she was searching for an answer to a question she hadn't yet asked. "I'm better. Thanks."

He nodded and waited for her to tell him why she was here. Instead, she reached into the pocket of her jeans and took out a handkerchief. Then timidly, like he was a horse that might bolt at any minute, she reached up and wiped his forehead. "You have oil all over your face," she said when he stepped back at her touch.

He raised his hand to take the handkerchief and met with her warm skin. She stepped closer until he could feel her breath on his face. She smelled like citrus.

"I missed you. I'm sorry I left like that." She closed her eyes and leaned her head against his.

He lowered their hands against his chest, knowing she would feel his heart pounding, then gently let her go when he couldn't think straight. "I missed you too." She seemed healthier now than she had. "How are you?"

Her lips curled. "I'm good. I got help in Longreach—it took a while, but I'm better now." There was a quiet pride to her voice. Like she had faced her demons and come out victorious. Which, he supposed, she had.

"Have you been flying again?"

She nodded. "I flew from Longreach. I've left my helicopter at Darcy's. Grant is back running the business again too. He's doing so well. Such an inspiration."

Noah's heart warmed. If Grant was anything like his cousin, he was too stubborn to let something like a wheelchair keep him from living a long, full life.

"How about you?" Riley asked. "What have you been doing?"

Waiting for you. "Working here with Lachie. He's started AA and has a sobriety sponsor."

"That's great. I'm happy for him."

He frowned at her. "Why are you here? Really?"

He watched her swallow and resisted the urge to place a kiss against that long, slender throat. "You once told me you loved me." Her voice was husky. "Do you think you could again?"

"I never stopped." He moved suddenly, capturing her lips and kissing her with a desperation and need that had been brewing for months. She matched his hunger, pushing her body against him and moving her hands over his back.

He pulled her with him to the privacy of the machinery shed and leaned her up against the corrugated iron wall. She moaned his name over and over as he kissed her face, ears, and neck.

Maybe if he were a stronger man, he could have held back, could have been more patient. But right now, all that mattered was making her his.

He moved his hands to her shoulders and ran them over her shirt, easing the buttons through the holes as he went. Every inch of skin that he exposed he had to cover with his mouth. He slowly drew her shirt up and off, and rediscovered the places that made her gasp with pleasure. When he finally lifted his mouth from her skin, his breath caught in his throat. "You're so beautiful."

With deft movements, he removed her bra and lowered his mouth to her breast and greedily sucked on a nipple. She moaned and arched into him, her hands threading into his hair and holding him closer. She moved against him, pure, sensual woman, and he drank in the sound of her shuddering breaths. The way she trembled with need. Noah wanted her so damn much. He wanted her so far beyond desire that it could only mean one thing.

With lips and hands, he caressed every inch of her skin

as he continued to undress her, sliding her jeans over her bottom and legs. He kneeled in front of her and slowly removed her boots and socks. Then her pants one foot at a time until she was naked in front of him.

He stayed kneeled in front of her but moved his gaze to her face. Their eyes locked.

"Noah." She sighed.

He kissed his way up her body before ravishing her mouth again.

"Please," she moaned, unbuttoning his shirt. He unzipped his jeans and pulled both his pants and underwear down to his ankles.

She wrapped her legs around his hips and Noah could hold back no longer.

He gave her his heart as he gave her his body, and the passion took them both. While their tongues danced together, their bodies were doing a dance of their own, slipping and thrusting and sliding and loving. As he sent her spiralling over the edge, she cried out his name again and tightened her grip around his hips. He buried his head in her neck as he joined her in ecstasy.

When his breathing evened out, he backed away so he could see Riley's beautiful face. He stroked her cheek and gazed into her eyes. She made a sound that reminded him of a cat purring.

"I love the way you love me." She kissed him tenderly and held his face between her hands. "I want us to try again, Noah. You're the one for me. I know it took me a long time to figure that out, but I know it now."

He kissed across her eyebrows and along her nose. "Better late than never." He grinned. "I love you, Riley."

"I love you too, Noah."

His heart swelled to the point where he was sure it would burst. He might not know what he wanted in his life, but he knew he wanted Riley in it. Wherever she went, he would go. They would work it all out, together.

EPILOGUE

"We better get going," Riley said, motioning to the helicopter behind her.

"Thanks for having me, Mum. I hope I wasn't too much hassle," Noah said with a grin.

Harriet McGuire remembered that grin from his childhood, before his father had used him for a punching bag. Riley had helped that grin return. Noah was finally the man he should always have been—confident and self-assured, with the love of a good woman.

"Thank you for coming. I'm glad everything is working out for you." She hugged her son as tears stung her eyes. "Don't be a stranger."

"We won't." Noah kissed her cheek and turned to his brother, Lachie. "Look after Mum."

Lachie slapped his brother on the shoulder. "She doesn't need looking after."

Riley kissed Harriet's cheek. "We'll see you soon."

Harriet wanted to tell the younger woman to fly safe and be careful, but she knew Riley was more than capable in the air and took safety very seriously. Noah would be in good hands with her as they explored and worked their way across the country. She had explained that Grant was looking after the business from Longreach and was finding them jobs in Western Australia. "Send me a post-card from Broome."

The lovebirds walked hand in hand over to the heli-copter, and Lachie put his big, strong arm around his mother's shoulders. "When are you going to find yourself a new bloke?"

Harriet laughed. "When you find a woman who will put up with you."

"Deal." Lachie squeezed her lightly.

Harriet smiled as the helicopter started up. Their family had been built on lies and torment, but her sons had grown to be good, decent men. Two had found the loves of their lives and Lachie? Well, Lachie would get there eventually. He was sober now and taking every day one step at a time.

She didn't know what the future held, although she suspected grandchildren from Meghan and Darcy wouldn't be too far off. Her children were the light of her life, and she was so grateful for them.

Riley and Noah waved from the cockpit before rising up off the ground in a flurry of dirt and wind. Harriet continued to wave even when she knew they could no longer see her. The dark blue helicopter got smaller and smaller, heading west for new adventures, leaving only Lachie and Harriet under the bright blue sky over Brigadier Station.

ALSO BY SARAH WILLIAMS

Brigadier Station Series:

The Brothers of Brigadier Station

The Sky over Brigadier Station

The Legacies of Brigadier Station

The Outback Governess (A Sweet Outback Novella)

Christmas at Brigadier Station (An Outback Christmas)

Heart of the Hinterland Series:

The Dairy Farmer's Daughter

For more information visit:

www.sarahwilliamsauthor.com

SARAH WILLIAMS

LOVE STORIES THAT WILL ROPE YOU IN

The Brothers of Brigadier Station

(#1 in the Brigadier Station series)

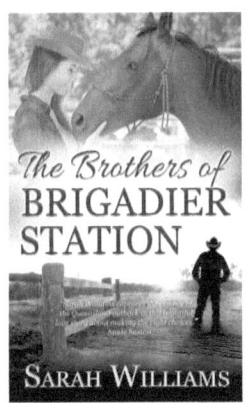

She came to the outback to marry the love of her life. She just didn't expect him to be her fiancé's younger brother.

When Meghan Flanagan, a vet-nurse from Townsville, moves to Brigadier Station in outback Queensland to marry the man of her dreams, she is shocked to discover that perhaps her fiancé isn't the man she wants waiting for her at the altar. The man she's destined to marry, just might be his younger brother.

Cautious of women after a disastrous past relationship, Darcy is happy living on his beloved cattle station, spending his spare time riding horses, going to rodeos and campdrafting. He didn't expect the perfect woman show up on his doorstep. Engaged to his brother.

With the wedding only hours away, Meghan must make the decision of a lifetime. But, her betrayal could tear the family apart. She knows all too well the pain of losing loved ones and being alone.

Now that she has the family she so desperately wants; will she risk losing it all?

Buy The Brothers of Brigadier Station

The Sky over Brigadier Station

(#2 in the Brigadier Station series)

He guards his heart. She yields to no man. Will a chance encounter set a course for true love?

Noah McGuire buries his demons deep inside. But when he's forced to return home to Brigadier Station to collect his inheritance, he can no longer avoid digging up his painful past. With the wounds of childhood trauma reopened, his world plunges into darkness until a beautiful pilot sets his heart afire.

Riley Sinclair isn't afraid to fly against the wind. While the spunky helicopter pilot's cattle herding business ruffles the feathers of most men, the handsome Noah seems different. But as demand for her skills grows, she worries that giving into passion could keep her dreams grounded.

As their chemistry soars, an unexpected tragedy throws their lives and their budding romance into a tailspin.

Can Noah and Riley leave their baggage behind to let love fly free?

The Sky over Brigadier Station is the second standalone book in the captivating Brigadier Station Western romance series. If you like flawed characters, simmering scenes, and stunning Australian and New Zealand settings, then you'll love Sarah Williams' rugged tale.

Buy The Sky over Brigadier Station

The Legacies of Brigadier Station

(#3 in the Brigadier Station series)

Can Lachie be the father Hannah needs? And the man Abbie deserves?

Lachie McGuire is trying to make a fresh start. He's sobered up and is making amends for all the people he has hurt and the pain he has caused. But some of his past actions have consequences. Even if he doesn't remember them.

Needing her independence, single-mum Abbie Forsyth accepted a nursing position in the small outback town of Julia Creek and uprooted her daughter, Hannah from the only life she had ever known. Now, in the dusty, sun burned land they are creating a life together, just the two of them.

When Lachie is injured and needs medical assistance, Abbie is there for him. She's by his side every step of the way, including letting him stay with them while he recovers from surgery. But Abbie knows how volatile life with an addict can be and she has to think about her daughter's safety above her own growing affection for the handsome grazier.

Then tragedy strikes the small rural town and secrets begin to unravel...

Return to the Outback for the third instalment in the bestselling Brigadier Station series.

Buy The Legacies of Brigadier Station

The Outback Governess

A Sweet Outback Novella

(#4 in the Brigadier Station series)

Can Paige bring the family back together or have the wounds of the past cut too deep?

When special-needs teacher Paige, takes up the position of Governess for three young children in the Queensland outback, she has no idea just how much and how quickly she would come to love the dusty, dry country, and the family who desperately need her.

Logan was heartbroken when his wife died, leaving him to raise their three children with the help of his aging parents on their remote cattle station. To avoid the constant reminder of the love he lost, he works on a mine in Mt Isa, meaning he only sees his family week on, week off.

But then tragedy strikes and Paige and Logan are forced to work together to look after the children, alone on the station. As well as being their teacher, Paige also becomes a substitute mother and teaches Logan how to be a parent again. A role he has avoided since losing his wife.

If you enjoyed The Brigadier Station series then you will love learning about distance education and how thousands of rural children are educated with the help of their parents and governesses.

The Outback Governess is a sweet, clean western romance by bestselling Australian author, Sarah Williams.

Buy The Outback Governess

The Dairy Farmer's Daughter

(#1 in the Heart of the Hinterland series)

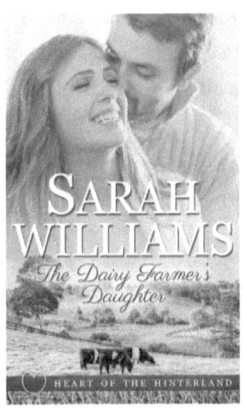

Will Justin choose riches over his heritage or will he find a love more valuable than all the money in the world?

Justin would have preferred to stay in the city and pretend it was an ordinary day. A day that didn't include a funeral for a father he'd barely known...

Justin Wheeler is not a country boy. He could have been, if his mother had stayed married to his father and not moved back to the city when he was only a toddler. But now that his estranged father is dead and he has inherited the dairy farm, Justin finds himself considering if the life he is living is actually the life he wants.

Family means everything to Freya Montgomery. She loves living on the land and helping to grow the family business. She knows how important agriculture is to their small hinterland community, so when Justin arrives in town and is offered a generous price from a housing developer to buy his property, Freya must convince him not to accept the deal and instead lease the land to her family.

The Dairy Farmer's Daughter is the first novella in an exciting new sexy, small-town series called "Heart of the Hinterland" by Bestselling author, Sarah Williams.

Buy The Dairy Farmer's Daughter

ABOUT THE AUTHOR

Bestselling author Sarah Williams spent her childhood chasing sheep, riding horses and picking Kiwi fruit on the family orchard in rural New Zealand. After a decade travelling, Sarah moved to Queensland to enjoy the endless summer, pristine beaches and tropical rainforests.

When she's not absorbed in her fictional writing world, Sarah is running after her family of four kids, one husband, two dogs, a horse and a cat.

She is Founder and CEO of Serenade Publishing, hosts the weekly podcast/vlog *Write with Love*, runs writers workshops and retreats, mentors and supports her peers to achieve their publishing dreams.

Sarah is regularly checking social media when she really should be cleaning.

To receive updates and free books, sign up for her mailing list.

www.sarahwilliamsauthor.com

facebook.com/sarahwilliamswriter

instagram.com/sarahwilliamsauthor

bookbub.com/profile/sarah-williams

goodreads.com/goodreadscomsarahwilliams

ACKNOWLEDGMENTS

To my best-buddy and talented writer friend Kelly Ethan - thank you for believing in me and this story.

My sincere thanks to all my writer friends who support and encourage me on this amazing journey. They include but are not limited to Kelly Ethan, Michelle Dalton and my incredible editor Lauren Clark.

To Myles Pollard for his amazing performance in the audiobooks.

A big thank you and much love to my family for all your support and for putting up with me while I write. I love you all.

And to you, dear reader. Thank you for choosing this book to read. I know there are many other distractions and entertainment options available these days, so thank you for joining Riley, Noah and me on this journey.

www.ingramcontent.com/pod-product-compliance
Lightning Source LLC
Chambersburg PA
CBHW021429110726
47901CB00008B/2357